ABOUT THE AUTHOR

Stephen Hodge has studied Atlantis and other lost civilisation myths for many years. He teaches Buddhism and
Tibetan language at the University of London and is the
author of several books including *The Piatkus Guide to
Tibetan Buddhism*.

Piatkus Guides

PIATKUS GUIDES

ATLANTIS

Stephen Hodge

PIATKUS

Published in the UK in 2000 by
Judy Piatkus (Publishers) Limited
5 Windmill Street
London W1P 1HF
e-mail: info@piatkus.co.uk

For the latest news and information on all our titles, visit
our website at www.piatkus.co.uk

The moral right of the author has been asserted
A catalogue record for this book is available from the British Library

ISBN 0-7499-2087-4

Page design by Paul Saunders
Edited by Rachel Connolly

Typeset by Action Publishing Technology Ltd., Gloucester
Printed and bound in Great Britain by
Mackays of Chatham PLC

CONTENTS

INTRODUCTION

The myth of Atlantis is probably the most enduring and well known of all the myths of the classical Mediterranean world. Forgotten by the Dark Ages of early medieval times, along with much of classical Greek and Roman culture, it was rediscovered around the time of Columbus's fateful voyage across the Atlantic Ocean. Since then the amount of literature on the subject has risen exponentially – some authorities claim the number of books published over the years which deal with the story of this vast, sunken continent and the mysterious civilisation lost under the sea exceeds five thousand!

As a child I was fascinated by the ancient cultures of the world, so much so that I used to spend most of my summer holidays in the galleries of the British Museum. I was enthralled by the Egyptians, and at one stage resolved to become an Egyptologist when I grew up. I also discovered the philosophy and literature of the

Greeks, which I distinctly preferred to anything that the humdrum Romans seemed to have produced. Later my horizons broadened and by virtue of some small talent for learning exotic languages I eventually became an orientalist, specialising in the languages and religions of India, China, Japan and Tibet. But I have maintained a keen interest in the latest archaeological finds around the world and what they can tell us about early human history. As a result I have kept up-to-date with the latest theories published concerning the whereabouts of the lost continent of Atlantis.

In this book, I have tried to present the most salient points in the long history of the Atlantis myth, from the thoughts of Plato himself to the latest theories of Graham Hancock. Naturally, I have had to be selective in the material I could include, and I must apologise in advance if I have not mentioned your favourite theory. I hope that what I have included is representative of the most important trends in the field. It is not always easy to reduce complex arguments down to a few paragraphs but I suggest that readers refer to the Further Reading section at the end of the book if they wish to explore any aspects in greater detail. I have also indicated the various difficulties that the many Atlantean theories throw up, though again readers should examine the validity of these arguments and counter-arguments for themselves.

In the course of my research for this book, I was frequently struck by something very strange. Although many Atlantis seekers are happy to theorise about the possible location of Atlantis, I was surprised to see that many authors either fail to quote the relevant dialogues of Plato, the *Timaeus* and the *Critias*, or only reproduce the parts of those dialogues which specifically deal with Atlantis itself. As a result, I believe that most people interested in Atlantis are unaware of the overall context in which Plato introduces the myth, a fact which clearly inhibits the possibility of coming to a balanced conclusion about the overall significance of the Atlantis myth. For example, I imagine that many readers will be surprised to find that the people and culture of Plato's Atlantis are not held up as an ideal super-civilisation. Quite the contrary – the Atlanteans are the villains of the piece for they are described as greedy, arrogant and aggressive. I would therefore recommend that, before plunging straight into this book, the reader obtains one of the various translations of the *Timaeus* and the *Critias*, and carefully reads what Plato himself actually said about Atlantis and the larger context of his story. Perhaps then, the matter of Atlantis will become clearer and easier to grasp.

1

PLATO AND ATHENS

ATHENS, 399 BCE

In a simple prison cell, an old but still vigorously healthy man with twinkling eyes is pacing up and down. He is surrounded by a group of care-worn friends barely able to hold back their tears. Most of his students are there, except for Plato who is feeling too sick to attend. He has spent the day talking to them, teaching them for one last time. But now the old man has drunk the hemlock poison and is waiting for its effects to begin working through his body. He chides his companions for their faint-heartedness.

'That's why I told the women to stay away! I thought you would do better – do be brave!'

The prison attendant feels the old man's legs and asks him if he still has any sensation there. Already the cold numbness has reached his thighs so he lies down on the bed, for now nature will take her course. He pulls the sheet over his head and, their tears exhausted, his friends stand around in silence. He uncovers his face one last time.

'We ought to offer a cock to Asclepius. See to it and don't forget.'

These were his last words, for moments later his body shuddered as his soul freed itself from its earthy home.

Thus died Socrates, of whom Plato later wrote, 'of all those whom we knew in our time, he was the bravest and also the wisest and most upright man'. How had Athens fallen so low that it would condemn and execute such a man on trumped-up charges? What had gone wrong with the greatest city in the Mediterranean that its people had become so unjust? Was there any chance of reforming the people and government so that this could never happen again? These questions were to haunt the heart-broken Plato for the rest of his life, and through his philosophy he built an enduring monument to Socrates. Just as Dante was so moved by his love of Beatrice that he went on to create a literary masterpiece, I believe it was primarily Plato's love for Socrates and his sadness at his death that eventually led him to produce the most influential set of philosophical writings the West has known; the early 20th-century philosopher A.N. Whitehead said that all of Western philosophy was nothing more than a series of footnotes to Plato. At the same time, the death of Socrates can also be seen as the genesis of Atlantis. To understand why this is so, we must go back to the late 6th century BCE and follow Athens' descent into decadence and injustice.

ASCENDANT ATHENS

At the beginning of the period under consideration, Athens was on its way to becoming the richest and most populated city in Greece, with its commercial and cultural influences spreading to many neighbouring cities. Like these other cities, Athens was a city-state – a city with a small surrounding area of countryside – for the dry, stony land of Greece did not readily favour the development of larger political units. Athens' main rival then and later was austere Sparta based in the southern Peloponnese.

Under the leadership of the great statesman Solon (640–560 BCE), Athens introduced the first tentative steps towards the form of government known as democracy, which gave all *free* male citizens of Athens the right to vote and hold office in Assembly and the ruling Council. Sadly, these attempts at reform were predictably sabotaged by various vested interests and rivalries. In rapid succession, power was seized first by conservatives, who ruled as an oligarchy by virtue of their wealth, and then by several powerful military men known as Tyrants. After the last of these, Hippias, was banished in 510 BCE, democracy was re-established with a reformed Assembly.

Yet waiting in the wings was the mighty army of the Persian Empire. The stories of their several attempts (512–450 BCE), to invade and conquer Greece under Darius and Xerxes and the heroic land and sea battles at Marathon, Thermopylai and Salamis that ensured Greek independence, are well known. Though the allied Greek city-states were ultimately victorious and drove the invaders from their land, Athens was taken and sacked by the Persians.

In this period of war that threatened to extinguish Greek independence forever, Athens played a key role, using its influence to expand beyond its traditional sphere of power. Under the rule of Pericles, this power was used wantonly to bleed dry the city's erstwhile allies, and the wealth used to rebuild Athens as a city of marvels. Almost unstoppable, the territory of Athens expanded across Greece.

THE PELOPONNESIAN WAR

Inevitably, in 457 BCE Athens and her allies went to war against their Spartan rivals for reasons that even now are somewhat unclear. Thus began the Peloponnesian War which dragged on for decades, with periodic truces being declared while the opponents paused to recover and regroup. It was during one of these short truces that Plato was born in 428 BCE.

At times during the war the Spartans had the upper

hand, even laying siege to Athens herself, while at other times Athens was in the ascendant. In 423 BCE, a group of influential moderates under Nicias eventually negotiated a truce with Sparta, though others such as Cleon attempted to carry on fighting. When Cleon was killed in 422 BCE, the famous Peace of Nicias was instituted. Athens took this opportunity to tighten her grip still further on her allies and colonies so that the city was by now an empire in all but name. But such greed and arrogance spelt trouble for Athens. In 415 BCE, an attempt was made under Nicias and Alkibiades to expand the territory of Athens into southern Italy where there were already several Greek colonies; the target of the invasion was Syracuse. The outcome was total disaster; the Athenians lost over 10,000 men and 200 ships. Alkibiades, a former student of Socrates, was partly blamed for the disaster and deserted to Sparta.

A GIANT FALLEN LOW

The Spartans saw their chance to deal with Athens once and for all and resumed hostilities. In Athens, the democratic government was overthrown and a group of conservative oligarchs known as the Four Hundred rose to power in 411 BCE, though they were eventually overthrown themselves because of their perceived links with the Spartans. The Athenian political merry-go-round then brought democracy back into favour, though it seems to have been little better than nationalistic mob-rule in the eyes of many.

Now, like a Greek tragedy, the final decline of Athens began. The dormant conflict with Sparta was fatally renewed. A series of military disasters followed, bleeding away manpower in defeat after defeat. Finally, in 404 BCE, Athens was obliged to surrender. Though the Spartans had wanted to raze Athens to the ground, reason prevailed. Instead, the city was left defenceless, her outer walls destroyed, and was ruled by a Spartan-nominated Assembly with strong oligarchic leanings. They were overseen by a pro-Spartan Council known as the Thirty Tyrants, which included one Critias – Plato's great-uncle (Critias IV). Though their rule lasted for little over a year, they unleashed a reign of terror during which many of their leading opponents were exiled or executed.

The pro-democracy populace revolted against the Thirty Tyrants. Many, like Critias, were killed outright or else driven out of Athens, while Sparta wisely chose not to get involved in the struggle. Once again, democracy was restored. In a little less than two hundred years, Athens had risen to dizzy heights of power and wealth only to plummet down again to a shadow of her former self. Such was the city in which Socrates lived and died, and in which Plato was raised and disappointed.

THE LIFE OF SOCRATES

During this time, a new group of innovative thinkers had arisen, a mixed bag of philosophers and the professional rhetorical speakers known as the Sophists. Socrates, who was born in 469 BCE, was taught by the Sophists but did not like the way they played hard and fast with words, in order to gain the upper hand. He became especially concerned with the question of truth and opinion – how were these to be distinguished? – and developed his famous method of questioning, uncovering the contradictions inherent in opinion and prejudice. He showed that though some people bandied around words like 'justice' and 'goodness', much as our politicians do today, they did not really understand what these words meant, nor did they use them consistently. He was also interested in many aspects of daily social life, summarised under the question, 'what is the good life?' – how can one best live a virtuous and happy life?

Socrates soon became popular with the young aristocrats such as Alkibiades, Critias, and later Plato himself. He would sit in the central square of Athens, the Agora, and teach his ideas to small groups of interested young men through penetrating argument and discussion.

Though famed as a philosopher, we must not forget that Socrates did not live in an intellectual ivory tower – he served bravely as a foot soldier at the battle of Delium in 424 BCE, for which he was decorated. Later, he also took an active, though sometimes reluctant, part in government during the time of the Four Hundred and served on the ruling Council when he made a stand for the rule of law against an angry mob.

THE TRIAL AND DEATH OF SOCRATES

Socrates lived and suffered, as many others did, through the turbulent years of the Peloponnesian War, yet when democracy was restored in 402 BCE his life was threatened from an unexpected quarter – Athens herself. When peace finally descended on a chastised and broken Athens, her citizens began to wonder why they had fared so badly, why the city's protector gods had failed them. Then, as people often do in such situations, they started looking for a scapegoat on whom they could lay the blame, while failing to see that they had brought all this upon themselves. Socrates' name began to be mentioned, for was it not he who had been friends with the traitors Alkibiades and Critias IV? Had he not upset the gods and the order of things by teaching his group of young admirers to challenge the assumptions of the age? Certainly, Socrates had irritated a number of people as he exposed their superficial and shoddy ways of thinking.

Finally, in 399 BCE, three opportunistic leaders, hoping perhaps to increase their own popularity with the mob, had Socrates indicted on the charges of refusing to recognise the gods of Athens and corrupting the youth. After a public trial, he was found guilty by the jury – made up of several hundred free Athenian citizens — and was sentenced to death. It is quite likely that those behind these trumped-up charges had hoped Socrates would quietly slip away into exile; certainly Socrates' friends urged him to do so. But as we know, he refused for he said he had always obeyed the laws of Athens no matter how inconvenient, and thus he drank the fatal hemlock.

PLATO'S EARLY YEARS

Plato was born into an old aristocratic Athenian family in 428 BCE, a few years before the short-lived Peace of Nicias was ratified between Athens and Sparta. Not much is known about Plato's early years, although it can be assumed that he was given a good education by tutors at home, as well as physical training in the gymnasium. While still young, he would have wandered around Athens, still a small city by modern standards, and must have encountered the short, bald man who held his small group of admirers spell-bound with his wit and acuity. It is quite possible that he accompanied his great-uncle Critias, or Charmides, his maternal uncle, to listen to Socrates, for Critias was one of Socrates' leading students.

As a young man, Plato was constantly seen in the company of the older Socrates, indeed, they were seen to have a very close relationship, though whether this implies a homosexual relationship in the modern sense is uncertain. Whatever the case, it is clear that Plato had a very deep love for Socrates that was to inspire his later philosophical writings. So when Socrates was condemned to death, Plato was profoundly shaken by the event. Judging from his later descriptions of Socrates, I am inclined to believe that Plato loved him more than any other living person, to the extent that he was too sick with grief and pain to attend the execution.

THE GUARDIAN OF SOCRATES' MEMORY

A short time after Socrates' death, Plato left Athens in disgust and went to the city of Megara where he met up with other Socratic friends. He spent a while travelling widely around the eastern Mediterranean, visiting Egypt and Cyrene. Eventually he returned to Athens in 395 BCE, where he served in the cavalry and saw some military action for which he was decorated. It seems that all this time he nursed his sense of loss and pondered how best Socrates should be remembered. Though Socrates had some successors, Plato probably felt that none of them was doing justice to the man he had known so well.

Perhaps it was around this time that Plato began writing his philosophical books. The first few, such as the *Apology*, were devoted to presenting his view of Socrates and his mentor's ideas. Plato's writings may seem like verbatim accounts of his teachings, but they are not, although he may well have made notes over the years when he was with Socrates, which he then rewrote as polished and initially accurate accounts of their conversations. In fact, all of Plato's writings have the appearance of realistic dialogues between Socrates and whoever else was present, but it must be understood that such dialogues were a recognised vehicle for presenting differing views in a dramatic and lifelike manner. It is well known that the later philosophical dialogues which depict Socrates owe little to the man himself, and are purely Plato's own compositions.

THE POLITICAL THEORIST

Once again, Plato was on the move. This time he made a trip to southern Italy in 388 BCE to visit the land of Pythagoras. He stayed a while in the region of Tarentum where many Pythagorean followers were settled. Here he had a number of important friends and picked up ideas from them that he was later to incorporate into his own philosophy. From Tarentum he sailed the short distance across to Syracuse in Sicily, a Greek-speaking but independent state. At that time, Syracuse was ruled by Dionysius, a rather short-tempered tyrant whose redeeming virtue was his love of poetry which he shared with Plato. Perhaps because Plato was a well-educated aristocrat and a poet to boot, he became mentor to Dionysius' brother-in-law, Dion. But like his master, Plato was outspoken against oppression and hypocrisy, and his distaste for tyrants in general soon came to the notice of Dionysius, who was understandably angered and ordered that Plato be expelled.

After many tribulations, including capture by pirates and enslavement, Plato eventually reached Athens safely. He then bought a small plot of land and set up the first formal school of philosophy for both young men and women. It was during these years in Athens that he is thought to have written his *Phaedrus*, *Symposium* and the seminal *Republic*. The *Republic* is a very long work and Plato's first attempt to describe the structure of an ideal state. The moral rectitude of this ideal state stands in stark contrast to what Plato had seen and heard of Athens over the decades. One of his key ideas was the concept of rule by a council of morally superior guardians who were to be trained in philosophy. Moreover, he thought that they in turn should be guided by an absolute philosopher-king – either a philosopher who has become king or a king who has become a philosopher. Perhaps underlying his desire to design the ideal city-state was the hope that never again would philosophers of Socrates' calibre be put to death to please the mob.

PLATO IN OLD AGE

In Syracuse, the old king Dionysius had died and his place taken by his son of the same name. In 367 BCE, Plato was invited by his old friend Dion to return and educate the young king, Dionysius II. Suddenly there seemed to be a heaven-sent opportunity for Plato to train somebody as his ideal philosopher-king. At first all seemed to go well, but inevitably court politics and jealousy undermined Plato's efforts. Plato left Syracuse, amidst recriminations, after seven years. By now he was getting old.

Returning to Athens, he began work on what he envisaged as a trilogy that would present a number of interconnected topics about the nature and history of the world and its inhabitants. He made use of some of the Pythagorean ideas he had adopted and, most critically for this book, a mythical account of Athens and Atlantis in a further attempt to describe an ideal city-state in motion. He wrote the first book, the *Timaeus*, in which the idea of Atlantis is briefly introduced, and then began but never finished the *Critias*, which expands in detail the Atlantis myth. Scholars are divided about Plato's reasons for abandoning this project. Perhaps he felt he had bitten off more than he could chew, or else he was merely dissatisfied with his efforts.

Plato made one more attempt to describe and refine his concept of the ideal city-state in his dry and somewhat disturbing work, the *Laws*. This was to be his last work before his death in 347 BCE. Little could Plato have suspected that within ten years of his death the very existence of all city-states in Greece would be abruptly ended with the conquest of the whole of Greece by Philip of Macedonia and his son, Alexander the Great.

2

THE ATLANTIS MYTH

Though many people have heard of the Atlantis story in some form or other, few have actually read Plato's account of Atlantis. Even when they have read Plato's own words, it is likely that they have only read the sections directly related to Atlantis in one of the many books written on the topic, and therefore out of their context. I have also found in my own research for this book that virtually all scholars specialising in Plato's philosophy are unanimous in their belief that the Atlantis myth is mere fiction. In contrast, it is the non-specialist, whether a person from another academic field or more usually an enthusiastic amateur without any appropriate expertise, who believes that the Atlantis myth refers to real historical events. When the latter are scorned by the specialists for their naivety, their reaction is to sneer at the short-sighted conservatism of the scholar.

As I have said, the context is everything. Perhaps one

way to understand the situation is to consider a gripping novel. As the writer works his or her magic, you may temporarily suspend your disbelief and become totally absorbed in the reality of what you are reading. But step back a little and common-sense tells you that you have been reading a book, a product of the writer's imagination. Your knowledge of the real world tells you that what you have read is merely fiction. But at the same time, a good novel does convey some sort of greater truth about life. In this sense, a work of fiction can also be said to be true. I shall return to this very pertinent question of truth later in this chapter, for the manner in which philosophers such as Plato understood truth is somewhat complicated.

ARCHAEOLOGISTS AND TREASURE-HUNTERS

Think of the myth of Atlantis as though it were an archaeological artefact. There are many amateur archaeologists who are little better than treasure-hunters, armed with spades and metal-detectors. If they find something of value, that is often all they are concerned with. They lift the object from the site and take it away with them to dispose of as they wish. True archaeologists raise their hands in horror at such irresponsible behaviour for they say that this destroys any meaning the object might have had. Taken out of its context in the ground, the object becomes stripped of all scientific meaning – often it can no longer be accurately dated.

Archaeologists can spend months on site, carefully sifting away the accumulated soil and debris, noting down the precise location of each object they find, photographing or drawing the article before it is removed and placed together with its companions for conservation. Later, the item can be subjected to a range of tests, comparisons made with similar objects from elsewhere, and so forth. In this way, a full picture of the object can be built up which throws light on all aspects of its manufacture, significance, use, and even its eventual loss centuries ago.

This is how I propose to approach the myth of Atlantis – examining each layer of the literary site in which it is found, though somewhat less painstakingly than an archaeologist working in the field. In this case, however, it will be easier to work outwards from the myth itself to its surrounds.

THE MYTH OF ATLANTIS

The myth of Atlantis is found in two of Plato's late works, the *Timaeus* and the *Critias*. It must be stressed that there is no mention whatsoever of this myth in the surviving writings of any other author before Plato. In each of these books, the 'characters' are the same: an idealised Socrates acting as Plato's mouth-piece; Critias III, Plato's great-grandfather; Timaeus the Pythagorean, who was probably modelled on one of Plato's friends from Tarentum; and finally Hermocrates, a Syracusan statesman and soldier who took part in the defeat of Athens' attack in 415 BCE.

In the first book, the Atlantis myth is only mentioned in passing before Timaeus, the character after whom the book is named, begins his Pythagorean account of cosmology and creation. The reference to Atlantis occupies just a few dozen lines. Critias relates a story he says he heard, mentioning that there was once a powerful confederation of kings who ruled over one large island known as Atlantis and many smaller islands located outside the Pillars of Heracles in the Atlantic Ocean. Atlantis also controlled large areas of Europe and Africa, bordering the Mediterranean. With their growing power and rapacity, the Atlanteans attempted to conquer the remaining free lands which included Greece. An alliance led by the Greeks defeated the Atlantean hordes and freed those who had been enslaved by them. Sometime later, all the Greek forces and the entire island of Atlantis were destroyed by a combination of violent floods and earthquakes.

The story of Atlantis is taken up again with an apparent wealth of detail in the *Critias*. Here there is basically the same story, but it is noteworthy that there is virtually no mention of the conflict between the Greek alliance and the Atlanteans, as there was in the *Timaeus* version. This time, Plato describes the layout of Atlantis and its capital, as well as the structure of its society, in great detail. He goes on to describe the gradual fall from grace as the members of Atlantean society became greedy and corrupt. A council of gods headed by Zeus is convened to decide the fate of Atlantis – and then suddenly the book breaks off, unfinished. It seems from the preliminary remarks at the start of the dialogue that it was the intention of Critias to give an account of human history down to the present day, but we shall never know what would have been included. It is a mystery why Plato failed to finish the book; the consensus among scholars is that he seems to have realised that his plan was too ambitious and would have been impossible to complete in a reasonable span of time, given that he was by this time an old man attempting to write his final testament for posterity.

THE MYTH OF ATHENS

Though it has received considerably less attention than the Atlantis myth, there is also the parallel though contrasting account of a mythical ancient Athens. Again, a very brief version is given in the *Timaeus*, but more details are to be found in the *Critias*. In the latter we are told how the gods divided up the world amicably amongst themselves and populated it with its inhabitants. Just like good shepherds, or perhaps the Guardians in Plato's *Republic*, these gods and goddesses nurtured the beings under their control through benign influence on their minds. Plato then goes on to say that Athene and Hephaestos had been allocated the land of Greece and created a race of good people for whom they set up the appropriate social institutions. Life in those days was hard and all their efforts were focused on survival. Various natural calamities gradually erased any accurate memories of the founders of the Greek civilisation, so, beyond a few names, knowledge of their achievements was lost; the people then were illiterate and did not have the leisure time to take an interest in their past.

Plato describes in detail the city and institutions of his ancient Athens – an Athens which he says existed over 9,000 years before his time. In many aspects, the social institutions of these ancient Athenians were conveniently similar to those Plato outlined in his *Republic*. Actually, Critias specifically states, 'in fact they followed in all things the regime we laid down yesterday when we were talking about our hypothetical Guardians'. Plato, through Critias, then explains that the land of Greece had originally been very fertile but later suffered extensive soil erosion through a series of natural disasters that reduced it to harsh barren land. After describing the layout of the ancient city, Plato tells us that the inhabitants of his idealised Athens again followed similar lives to his *Republic* citizens. They were well organised, frugal and disdained extravagant wealth; moreover they were such true pillars of moral rectitude that the rest of Greece recognised them as the natural leaders of the entire land.

SOLON

The next layer that envelops the myths of Atlantis and ancient Athens is Plato's account of their origin.

According to Critias III, Plato's spokesman in the *Timaeus* and the *Critias*, it was the great Greek statesman Solon (c. 640–560 BCE) who heard the story of Atlantis in Egypt and brought it back to Athens. As discussed in Chapter 1, Solon was famous for his political and economic reforms designed to make the city-state of Athens more democratic; among other things, he is said to have extended the civic franchise to persons who had previously been excluded. He is also known to have been interested in ancient history and prehistory, for he actually used archaeology to prove that the island of Salamis had originally been Athenian territory by excavating ancient graves and showing that they had been buried in the Athenian style rather than that of Megara, the rival claimant.

It should also be noted that Solon was an ancestor of Plato himself and was admired by Plato as an outstanding example of a doer, a man of action, rather than the type of idle poet he so disdained.

Solon probably visited Egypt as an old man in his fifties around 590 BCE, soon after he had enacted his reforms. The account given by Plato does not specify the precise dates of Solon's visit but tells us that Solon was staying in the Nile Delta city of Sais, which by that late stage of Egyptian history had become the capital. It is known that many Greeks were settled in parts of the Delta, with a free port at nearby Naucratis. Indeed, it is possible that the city of Sais had been partially founded by Greek visitors many centuries before, for, according to Plato, the inhabitants 'are very friendly to the Athenians and claim some relationship with them'.

THE EGYPTIAN CONNECTION

It seems that Solon was discussing Greek history and myths with some Egyptian priests and was surprised that the Egyptians were somewhat dismissive of Greek knowledge of the past. He was told that mankind was periodically destroyed by catastrophic floods and fires, and that the majority of people in other countries would perish. In this way, records and knowledge of the past were lost to them. The Egyptians, on the other hand, were spared such catastrophes because of the natural conditions prevailing in Egypt. Conveniently, they alone had preserved detailed records of the past and hence knew of things that nobody else remembered.

The priest said that a record concerning an ancient Athens and her rival Atlantis was carved on a pillar and preserved in Egypt, and recounted myths of Athens and Atlantis to Solon, though whether from memory, a papyrus transcription or the actual pillar is unclear. He said that the founding of Egypt dated back to a time 8,000 years previously (8500 BCE). We know from orthodox archaeology, however, that this date is a gross exaggeration, since the date for the emergence of the Egyptian state cannot be much earlier than 3100 BCE.

The priest told Solon that Athens was in existence 1,000 years before the kingdom of Egypt, around 9500 BCE. It seems that Greek pride had to be gently massaged and given the credit of being the senior civilisation, though again archaeologically we know that this is sheer fantasy; the true date would seem to be 2100 BCE, when the Minoan and Mycenaean cultures emerged. The priest also told Solon that the empire of Atlantis was founded around the same time as that of Athens.

Regardless of the truth concerning the founding dates of the Athenian, Atlantean or Egyptian cultures, there are several noteworthy problems about the priest's account as supposedly related to Solon. First, we are accustomed to a continuous system of dating. There is a starting point, the traditional year of the birth of Jesus, from which we count either forwards or backwards. Ancient people did not have any such system. Several methods were used, the most common being the dates of the succession of kings. The dates would start with the accession of a king to the throne and continue until his successor took over.

This system was in use in Egypt and has given rise to much confusion in Egyptian chronology, both in ancient times and today, as is becoming apparent through the work of such scholars as David Rohl. From time to time, dynasties of pharaohs reigned in parallel in the north and the south of Egypt, and not successively as it seems from the existing records. For example, the total regnal lengths of one block of pharaohs may have been 150 years, while that of another concurrent block may have been 100 years. The mistake made in the past was to treat these as successive dynasties, thus giving the erroneous total of 250 years when it should be just 150. This has serious implications for the ability of the priest to accurately date for Solon those events which happened in the distant past.

Even if we suppose that these dates are accurate, another problem is that the date given by the priest for the founding of the Egyptian state is, in modern terms, 8500 BCE. That is 1,000 years after the events described in the Atlantis/Athens myth. How are those events supposed to have been transmitted to the Egyptians, given that the priest told Solon that all other peoples lost their records through periodic catastrophes and cannot remember their past? Similarly, the priest implied that the Egyptians kept meticulous records from the founding of the country in 8500 BCE, but again this is mere fantasy in view of the fact that the earliest fragments of the characteristic Egyptian hieroglyphic script, as it was still being developed, do not date much earlier than 3000 BCE. The priest also told Solon that the Egyptians were careful to record details of world events as they happened for posterity, yet surviving Egyptian records do not substantiate this. In fact, apart from a few short periods such as during the Eighteenth Dynasty in the 11th century BCE, the Egyptians seem to have been totally uninterested in world events!

THE GENEALOGY OF THE MYTH

It is not known in what form Solon was told the story of the ancient war between Athens and Atlantis and the subsequent disaster that befell them. That is to say, was it from written sources that were translated for him on the spot, or did the priest merely tell him the story from memory? Presumably, if we are to believe Plato's account, Solon would have made some notes, either as the priest spoke or shortly afterwards. Through Critias, Plato tells us that Solon wanted to use the material for a didactic poem which he failed to complete because affairs of state needed his attention. Like Plato, Solon was also famed as a poet, though he was first and foremost a statesman, concerned with ordering or reforming society.

Plato did not have a high opinion of poets in general for a number of reasons, but one of his main objections to their craft was that they wrote of matters about which they did not have first-hand knowledge – they used their imagination and, lacking wide experience of the world, they diminished or falsified their subjects. Although Solon could write passable poetry, he was experienced in the ways of the world and had the knowledge of one who does things rather than talks about them. Solon also had a reputation for honesty which Plato plays on in his presentation of the Atlantis/Athens story as a way of giving it credibility.

So Solon had the unfinished poem and perhaps some notes about the myth in his possession. Knowledge of the myth, Plato's narrator Critias says, was passed down through the family for several generations. Critias, we must remember, was in real life Plato's great-grandfather – Critias III in the genealogy (see fig. 1). He claims to have been told the story when he was a child of no more than ten years of age by his grandfather, Critias II, who was a nephew of Solon. We do know that Solon did pass some poetic material on to his nephew, because one surviving fragment of another poem is addressed to this Critias. However, though the genealogy of the story down to Critias III seems superficially plausible, it too has problems.

Reading carefully what Critias says, he seems unable to make up his mind whether he is telling the story from childhood memory or by reference to a manuscript. Given the amount of detail in the accounts of ancient Atlantis and Athens, is it really credible that a ten-year-old child could have remembered the information accurately? Even if he had remembered the story as he was supposed to have been told it by his grandfather, how did the story get into Plato's hands? Don't forget that Plato is writing here about a conversation between Critias and Socrates that took place when he was a mere infant.

Of course, some writers on the Atlantis myth have suggested that Plato himself might have inherited family documents that he referred to for details of the myth, but this seems unlikely. If you look back at the overview of Athenian history and note the succession of wars and

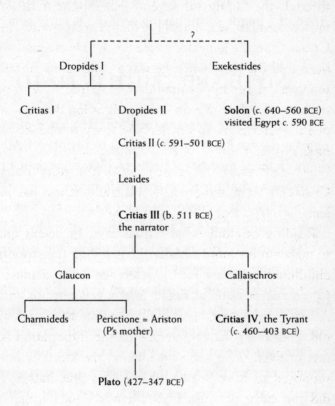

Plato's genealogy

destruction that took place between the time of Solon and Plato's old age, I think you will agree that the likelihood of a fragile scroll having survived is fairly slim.

MYTH AND TRUTH IN PLATO

It is now possible to place the entire sequence of events against the backdrop of the turbulent history of Athens, while looking at other aspects of Plato's account of the myth and enquiring as to what it all means.

Once again it is important to look at the context of the story. Regardless of the truth of the myth, why is Plato telling it to us? The answer is very simple and is given in the opening dialogue of the *Timaeus*, which is normally omitted in books on the Atlantis myth. At the opening of the book, Socrates summarises a discussion that is supposed to have taken place the previous day concerning the structure of the ideal state that is so highly reminiscent of that given in the *Republic*. In Socrates' view, what he has described is a static account of an ideal city-state, but now he wants it to be set in motion by some example. 'There are conflicts which all cities undergo, and I should like to hear someone tell of our own city carrying on a struggle against her neighbours, and how she went out to war in a becoming manner, and when at war showed by the greatness of her actions and the magnanimity of her words in dealing with other cities a result worthy of her training and education'.

This hints at a difficulty Plato had experienced with his ideal city-state in the *Republic*, namely that the possibility of establishing such a city-state should not be dismissed merely because there are no actual examples of such a place having existed. Socrates wants to hear about his ideal citizens in action but does not necessarily demand that such an account be historical, merely that the example accords with the ideals he has set forth. Indeed, Socrates suggests in the *Republic* that the stories which might be told about the past can be taken as useful inventions. But if a philosopher constructs such stories for didactic reasons in the absence of real historical knowledge, the truth to which he likens his story cannot be historical in the accepted sense.

On several occasions in the two dialogues, Critias is most insistent that the story he is telling is the truth, no matter how far-fetched it may seem to his audience. Many writers on Atlantis have taken Plato's words at face-value and have thus assumed that the story must be true. But as we have seen, the account he gives of the Atlantis/Athens myth seems implausible, so is there some other explanation for this insistence upon the veracity of the story?

When we say something is true, we normally mean that it is factual or real. So what would Plato have meant when he used the word 'true'? Of course, he would have understood our definition of truth, but he would also have used the word in contexts that are unfamiliar today. For Plato, even myths may at times be true even though they refer to palpably fictitious events. For example, if in a myth Zeus punishes an evil person, then that is true because it corresponds to what is known about the character of Zeus as a just being. On the other hand, if Zeus acts in a way that is out of character, then such a myth must be false. On these grounds, Plato dismissed most myths as false because they were written by poets who did not have the training or knowledge that would have enabled them to construct true myths.

Although Critias's account of Solon's story is not written as poetry, it has some of its typical characteristics, for Critias also states, 'All that is said by any of us can only be imitation and representation'. It is likely, therefore, that Plato wants people to understand his story as a philosophical poem about how good men would behave, contrasting Athens to Atlantis, rather than the dubious type of myth that he treated with disdain for its lack of veracity. Plato also wants to present the citizens of his ideal city-state in the most convincing manner; he wants us to believe that such a city-state is possible and to see the benefits it yields for its inhabitants. To convince us of this, he uses several devices which seem to add plausibility to the account, while at the same time subtly hinting that it is, after all, only a didactic story.

For example, he has Critias claim that his story is valid because it comes from ancient records kept in Egypt. Though you might not see anything untoward in this, it would have alerted the Greek reader to the true state of affairs surrounding the story. For although the

Greeks had a great admiration for Egyptian culture and were well aware of its antiquity, they also had a stereotypical idea of Egyptians as devious liars, 'wily Orientals', ever ready to cheat the upright and honest Greek visitor. Plato even states this explicitly in his *Laws*, when he says that the Egyptians of his time lacked true wisdom but excelled in 'knavery'. Any Greek reader would therefore expect a story told by them to be deceitful, and in this way Plato is hinting that the story should not be taken literally.

Plato is happy to use the story, however, if it serves a greater end through the veracity of the characters of its protagonists. In fact, Plato approved of such 'noble lies', as he tells us in the *Republic*, 'Now, we can devise one of those lies – the kind which crop up as occasion demands, which we were talking about not long ago – so that with a single noble lie we can indoctrinate the rulers themselves ... Nothing outlandish, just a tall story.' In this passage, Plato literally says 'a Phoenician story.' and all Greeks knew that Egyptians were just like the Phoenicians – devious tricksters who were clever at coming up with useful stories that philosophers used to their advantage.

To make his story seem even more plausible, Plato packs his account of Atlantis with detail and thus uses another device that non-specialist readers today can easily overlook. Most will be unaware that the word 'detail' or 'precision' is a technical term used by the new school of Greek historians around the time of Plato.

Earlier historians like Herodotus were indiscriminate in the way they mixed fact with legend and myth, whereas the new type of historian, represented by people such as Thucydides, wanted precision and accuracy and this they believed could only be provided for recent events. Thus the historian Ephorus stated, 'On contemporary events we regard as the most believable those who give the most detailed account. On events in the distant past, however, we consider such an account wholly implausible on the grounds that it is unlikely that all actions and most speeches would be remembered over so long a period of time'. And this is just the problem with Plato's account of ancient Atlantis and Athens – how could the details have been handed down accurately over the centuries before the Egyptians recorded them? By over-emphasising his pretence to historicity, surely Plato is actually hinting at its fictionality.

THE PURPOSE OF THE MYTH

So what was Plato's reason for inventing this story? If you consider the matter carefully, there are several possible reasons. Of course, his primary purpose was to make people believe in the possibility of events they would not believe to be possible in the present. In his comments on hearing the story, even Socrates is implicitly sceptical about it when he says, 'Where shall we find an alternative if we abandon it? No, you must tell it and good luck to you!' In other words, Socrates is being ironic in saying how convenient it is that this story pops up just when needed. It is a wonderful and convenient vehicle for demonstrating how the ideal citizens of the proposed city-state would behave in real life.

Another purpose of the story becomes clear if Athenian history is taken into consideration. As seen in Chapter 1, Plato had little reason to respect the Athens of his time – she had become venal, arrogant, and, worst of all, she had condemned Plato's beloved Socrates to death. The story of Atlantis and Athens was therefore intended to parallel two sets of events in Athenian history. In the first case, the morally upright Athens of the myth represents Athens at the time of the Persian Wars, while Atlantis, naturally, corresponds to the powerful yet morally corrupt Persian Empire. Just as Athens in the conflict with Atlantis led a Greek alliance to victory, so also did Athens against the Persian hordes. Though numerically inferior to the Persians, it was Greek moral superiority that granted them victory.

However, the myth was also used cleverly as a veiled criticism of Plato's contemporary Athens. By then, the Athenians had taken on the attributes of the Atlanteans and had become the arrogant aggressors lacking in moral rectitude, while it was the Syracusans who were morally superior and thus carried the day to Athens' cost. In other words, Plato probably envisaged his work as a warning to his fellow Athenian citizens to abandon their love of wealth and power and to return to his idealised past.

Instead of using poor Socrates as their scapegoat, the Athenians ought to have looked to their own failings and realised the true reason that their gods had apparently abandoned them.

3

THE ATLANTIS MYTH
REKINDLED

OTHER TRACES OF ATLANTIS?

I have suggested that the myth of Atlantis is purely a product of Plato's mind, though many will disagree. Yet the fact remains that Plato was the only writer in the ancient Mediterranean world, as far as is known, who spoke of the destroyed island or continent of Atlantis, though it is true that various writers allude to certain tribes whose name is reminiscent of Atlantis. For example, the historian Herodotus, who lived some hundred years before Plato, mentions a primitive tribe living in North Africa known variously as the Atalantes, the Atarantes or the Atlantioi. These people are clearly named after Atlas, the giant of Greek mythology who was thought to support the heavens upon his shoulders. His abode was thought to lie somewhere in North Africa among the mountains that are still known as the Atlas Mountains, but that area of North Africa lay well away from the sphere of Greek knowledge and was also thought to be populated by various other mythical beings.

The encyclopaedist Diodorus of Sicily (fl 60–30 BCE) who compiled a great mass of valuable information derived from earlier authors in his *Historical Library*, also mentions the Atlantioi in passing. He tells of a Queen Myrina of the North African Amazons, who first subjugated the Atlantioi and then aided them in defeating the neighbouring tribe, the Gorgons. But these Atlantioi were clearly a primitive people who apparently had no language of their own and had little connection with the Atlantis of Plato beyond a similarity of names.

Other writers mention some islands in the Atlantic such as Ogygia and Aiaia, but again these have no obvious connection with Atlantis and are possibly references to the Azores, Canaries or Madeiras, which were known to the seafaring Phoenicians living in Carthage. All in all, there is nothing to indicate that an account of the lost lands of Atlantis was known to anybody prior to Plato's telling of the story.

THE LATER CLASSICAL WRITERS

How did Plato's contemporaries react to his story? Unfortunately, it is impossible to say with certainty for no relevant writings have survived to the present day, although the geographer Strabo (63 BCE–23 CE) reveals that most of Plato's fellow intellectuals viewed the Atlantis story as a fictitious social allegory or, at best, were noncommittal about its veracity. Even Plato's chief disciple Aristotle, who was with him for many years and therefore in a position to know the truth of the matter, does not mention Atlantis once in his wide range of studies. Strabo reports, however, that Aristotle said ironically, 'just as Homer had been compelled to erect the wall of the Achaeans around their ships on the beach at Troy and then to wash it away, so also in the case of Atlantis, he who invented it also destroyed it'.

Apart from Aristotle, the only other near contemporary who commented on the story was Crantor, an early follower of Plato. It seems that he did believe in the literal truth of Atlantis and, possibly to defend his master's reputation, he made a trip to Sais in Egypt where he was allegedly shown the same pillar that Solon had seen.

Marcellus, a geographer who was active around 100 BCE, produced a work known as the *Ethiopic History*, though this is now unfortunately lost. It is known, however, that he mentioned three large and seven small islands located in the Atlantic and reported that their inhabitants preserved the traditions of Atlantis and its empire. He may, however, have been referring to the Azores, Canaries and Madeiras, and would have been quite familiar with Plato's account of Atlantis.

Somewhat later, during the Roman period, the views of scholars and philosophers were much the same – scepticism from some, acceptance from others. In fact the

Jewish philosopher, Philo of Alexandria, wanted to have it both ways since he stated that the story was both allegorical and also literally true! The Roman writers Pliny and Elder and Plutarch, mentioned Plato's story in their writings but in somewhat sceptical terms. And Proclus, a leading neo-Platonist and commentator on the works of Plato, also tended to be sceptical about the literal truth of the Atlantis story for he said that 'Critias had woven a myth worthy of the festival of the Lesser Panathenaia', a festival in honour of Athene which was in progress at the time of the dialogue. Yet there were some who did lean towards cautious acceptance of the story, such as the Stoic philosopher Poseidonos, the tutor of Cicero, who wrote that 'it is possible that the story about the island of Atlantis is not a fiction', on account of the known effects of earthquakes and erosion which are also mentioned in Plato's account.

Though the early Church Fathers such as Origen and Porphyrius considered the story to be an allegory concerning the struggle between good and evil, most of the later Fathers were quite uncritical in their acceptance of the account as it suited their own agendas. One of the last people in ancient times to have commented on the story was the 6th-century reactionary Egyptian monk known as Cosmos Indikopleutes, who employed considerable mental gymnastics in his assertion that the Atlantis myth upheld the then current Christian idea that the world was flat, while maintaining that the myth was merely a distorted version of the Flood.

It must have been around this time that people in the Mediterranean area lost interest in the ideas of Plato as the last pagan philosophers died out. Indeed, virtually all Greek writings, philosophy included, became inaccessible around this time in Western Europe as ties with the eastern Mediterranean weakened. After this time, until the rediscovery of Plato's works in the late medieval period, the *Timaeus* was the only work by Plato to be transmitted to the West via the Latin translation by Chalcidius. The very last mention of Atlantis in these early times is said to be in the encyclopaedia compiled by the early 12th-century Honorius of Autun.

EUHEMERUS

Before leaving the ancient world, I would like to draw your attention to a little known writer, Euhemerus, who lived about 100 years after Plato. Few details are known about him, including the exact dates of his life, but he was employed as a kind of philosopher/historian in the court of Cassander. Cassander took the Macedonian throne after the death of Alexander the Great; it was at his hands that Alexander's wife Roxana and his son were murdered. Unlike Alexander the Great, who travelled and conquered vast tracts of land from Greece to the borders of India, Cassander was a nobody with a chip on his shoulder. He did all he could to counter the memory of Alexander, or else made feeble attempts to outshine his illustrious predecessor. However because Cassander lacked the means and the ability to equal Alexander's journey to the East, scholars believe that he devised a surrogate means of doing so.

This is where Euhemerus played his part through his lost book, the *Sacred History*, which is known only through the lengthy extracts preserved by Diodorus of Sicily. This work purports to be an account of a visit to a utopian island known as Panchaea, located somewhere along the coast of Arabia Felix. While he was there, Euhemerus claimed to have found columns inscribed with historical accounts of ancient kings named Zeus, Cronos and Uranus, among other things. He claimed that some of the inscriptions had come from Greece, some from Panchaea itself, while others had come from far away Sri Lanka. Though people may have given credence to his statements, it is clear to a modern reader that most of the accounts of his distant travels and his findings resemble an ancient version of *Gulliver's Travels*.

Euhemerus himself would have been forgotten long ago but for an interesting approach he took with respect to his material. He believed that the various ancient gods such as Zeus were really outstanding men who had been commemorated for their contributions to culture by being deified. In other words, he believed that myths had their origins in actual events and were transmuted into myths over the course of centuries by ignorant people. It is curious that this euhemeristic approach, as it is known, should be echoed in the writings of some present-day researchers in their attempts to unravel the mysteries of the ancient world. Perhaps Euhemerus should be enshrined as their patron deity!

ATLANTIS REDISCOVERED?

A dark veil descended over the Atlantis story for many centuries, though it was perhaps more dormant than dead. However, as European seafaring skills gradually improved, the myth once again sprang to life.

By the early 15th century, some mariners had become obsessed with the holy grail of navigation – the transatlantic route to the lands of the East, the source of gold and spices. In addition, some scholars have recently hypothesised that medieval Basque and English fishermen made regular secret trips across the north Atlantic to the Newfoundland area for the cod that abounded in the seas off those coasts. They argue that this knowledge was kept secret since cod, when dried, was an extremely valuable commodity in medieval Christian Europe, with its many fast-days when the consumption of meat was forbidden.

Whatever the truth of this, the credit for 'discovering' the Americas went to the Genoan adventurer Christopher Columbus. Because of Columbus's apparent confidence that he would find land at the end of his journey across the Atlantic, it has been suggested that he must have had some prior knowledge of the relatively close proximity of land. Perhaps, some have theorised, he had heard of the voyages made by the cod fishermen, while others suggest he may well have been familiar with the writings of Plato which were becoming known to west European scholars again.

Atlantis in the Americas

Whether Columbus was inspired by Plato's account of Atlantis will doubtless remain a mystery, yet his discovery of America and its exploration by his immediate successors rekindled interest in the Atlantis story, for some way had to be found to account for the indigenous population. It was the Spanish who were most active in the newly discovered continent for they soon extended their dominion over much of Central America and parts of South America.

Although the existence of the native inhabitants of the Americas was obviously known from the moment Columbus set foot on the islands of the Caribbean, Europeans were initially uninterested in the culture or history of these unfortunate people, who were frequently enslaved, massacred, infected with deadly, contagious diseases, or at best forcibly converted to Christianity. Despite the powerful impression that the literate Aztec and Mayan urban cultures of Central and South America initially made on the travelling colonists, the good Christian priests and friars wasted no time in burning vast amounts of native literature while greedy, rapacious soldiers destroyed the cities and towns. It was only after some decades that European scholars, usually priests, made a calmer appraisal of the discoveries and began to reflect upon the culture and history of their victims.

One of the first comprehensive accounts of the Spanish exploits in the Americas was written by Francisco Lopez de Gómara. Born in 1510, he was ordained a priest and later became the private and domestic chaplain of Hernando Cortés, the foremost of the conquistadores, who overthrew the Aztec empire, murdered its ruler Montezuma and completely destroyed the capital Tenochtitlan which stood on the site of present-day Mexico City. Gómara himself did not have the good fortune to accompany his illustrious patron to America, but nevertheless took a keen interest in events. As chaplain to Cortés, he would have had access to various eye-witness accounts of the Spanish conquest of the Aztecs and these formed the basis of a general history of the Spanish in the Indies and Mexico, the *Hispania Victrix*.

It was in this book that the influential idea first emerged that the Atlantis of Plato was nothing other than an account of America from earlier times. This idea was to be strengthened when the Spanish subsequently revealed that the Aztecs had related that they had long ago migrated from a semi-mythical place called Aztlan – the Place of Cranes – from which the name 'Aztec' derives. The Aztecs described their ancient homeland as an island surrounded by reeds within a lagoon, though its exact location had been hotly debated; it was probably somewhere in the highlands to the north-west of Tenochtitlan.

Nevertheless, the idea that the ancient Aztec homeland was Atlantis was further enhanced when it was found that the common Nahuatl (Aztec) word for 'water' was *'atl'*! This theory about the origin of the Aztecs continues to attract supporters even today.

Such was the excitement at the possibility that the location of Atlantis, or at least part of it, had been found in the Americas, that in 1561 Guillaume de Postel wanted to give the name Atlantis to an area of the Americas. Before the Atlantic had been thoroughly explored in this era of relatively primitive navigation, it was even thought

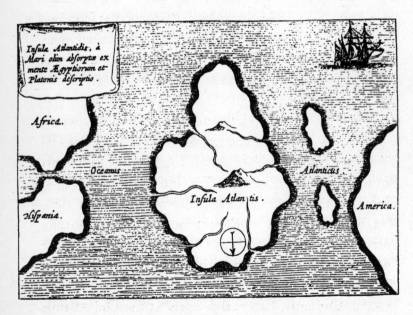

The first known map of Atlantis, according to Athanasius Kircher, 1665

that Atlantis was still visible in the ocean and was thus shown on various maps, though these have all long since been handed over to museums and archives. Among them is the famous map by the Jesuit polymath Athanasius Kircher, in his *Mundus Subterraneus* (1644), in which Atlantis is located lying in the north Atlantic between America and Europe. There is also the generally reliable map of Ortellius, published in 1570, which shows a number of fictitious islands dotting the north and south Atlantic, such as the Isle of Brazil, St Brendan's Island, the Isle of the Seven Cities, the Green Island, the Island of the Demons, Vleanderen, Drogio, Emperadada, Estotiland, Grocland and Frisland. Of these, the fictitious Isle of Brazil, thought to be located a few hundred miles west of Ireland, enjoyed particular longevity, for it was finally removed from all maps only in the early years of the nineteenth century.

In addition to these early attempts to physically locate Atlantis, the idea was once again influential as a social allegory. The Elizabethan period saw a revival of interest in utopian societies both in England and in the rest of Europe. One such example is the *Utopia* of Thomas More (1516), which does not mention Atlantis specifically although More's happy land is an island situated in the West. Directly influenced by Plato's Atlantis was Francis Bacon's work *The New Atlantis*, which he located in the Pacific. Curiously, Bacon also refers to the Old Atlantis which he locates in the Americas. Some writers who believe that Atlantis was really situated in America have postulated that Bacon must therefore have had access to secret documents while he was studying in Oxford.

THE MAYA

Centred on the south Mexican peninsular of Yucatan and Guatemala, there once flourished another advanced Central American civilisation, the Maya. The area is still inhabited by the fiercely independent descendants of the early Mayan culture first encountered by the Spanish in the 16th century, though much of their cultural heritage has sadly been swept away. Like their Aztec neighbours further to the north, the pre-modern Maya developed a highly sophisticated urbanised civilisation. They were also literate and once possessed many thousands of their characteristic fan-folded books in their temple and palace archives. Today only four of these survive, thanks once again to the destruction wrought upon these people in the name of Christianity. Tragically, most of the books were burnt before it even occurred to anybody to learn how to read them. Yet, like so many conquerors elsewhere, the Spanish seemed to have a schizophrenic approach to their new subjects, prompted perhaps by their guilty consciences. One such typical individual was Diego de Landa.

Diego de Landa was a Spanish monk who accompanied the conquistadores to Central America in the 1560s and made himself so useful in the service of the Church that he eventually became Bishop of Yucatan, the former heartland of the Mayan civilisation. Like so many of his kind, he was responsible for burning huge amounts of Mayan literature in the belief that they contained diabolical teachings or mere pagan superstition. But, strangely, he seems to have had a slight change of heart towards the Maya and so tried to learn the Mayan writing. At that time, most Europeans were unfamiliar with the various possibilities of recording speech, for the decipherment of other ancient scripts such as the Egyptian hieroglyphs or the Mesopotamian cuneiform lay many centuries away. It is hardly surprising then that Diego de Landa assumed that Mayan was written using an alphabet, in the same way as the European languages with which he was already familiar. Interrogating his Mayan informants, he listed what he thought was the Mayan alphabet. Of course, his findings were largely nonsensical, though he went on to publish them in his very influential *Relacion de las Cosas de Yucatan* (*An Account of the Affairs of Yucatan*).

Diego de Landa also promulgated an interesting theory about the origins of the Maya. He said that he had heard from some Mayan elders in Yucatan that the land was first inhabited by some people 'who came from the East whom God had delivered by opening twelve paths through the sea'. Upon hearing this, it immediately became obvious to him who these ancestors were, for he continues, 'if this were true, it necessarily follows that all the inhabitants of the Indes are descendants of the Jews'. This wild but influential theory was to gain many supporters over the centuries thereafter, such as William Penn and even Oliver Cromwell, with some still holding such views until recent years.

Reading Mayan

Within a few decades of the Spanish invasion of the Mayan homelands, the knowledge of the Mayan script faded as the traditional culture collapsed and roman script was universally adopted in the region. During the 19th century, interest was awakened in the few enigmatic books that survived. At this time museums were filling up with spoils from sites all over the world, and the first scientific archaeologists were excavating the lands of Egypt and the Fertile Crescent in Mesopotamia. All the major scripts of the ancient Near East had largely been deciphered and so some turned to more obscure areas. The Mayan script attracted the attention of the French scholar, the Abbé Charles-Etienne Brasseur (1814–1874). He managed to get access to a copy of Diego de Landa's Mayan alphabet and thought he could use it to translate the Mayan writings. To his credit, he was successful in identifying some components of Mayan writing, such as the numerical system, some of the signs for the days, and so forth. But on the whole, what transpired from his efforts was little better than outlandish nonsense since Landa's so-called alphabet was nothing of the sort.

It is now known that the Mayans wrote with a system somewhat similar to the Egyptians and the Sumerians, using a combination of ideograms and phonetic elements, and most of Mayan writing can now be read thanks to the efforts of the Russian scholar Yuri Knorosov. The ideograms are stylised representations of objects, each used as a rebus with further meaning added by purely phonetic elements. To illustrate how this works, take a simple sentence in English: I saw the cat. If we used the Mayan way of writing, we would have a picture of an eye, followed by a picture of a saw, and finally a picture of a cat with the word 'the' perhaps written phonetically.

To return to Brasseur's efforts, while 'reading' one Mayan book, the *Codex Troano*, using Landa's alphabet, he thought he had identified the name of an ancient land that had been, according to his translation, destroyed by floods and earthquakes. He read, 'The master is he of the upheaved earth, the master of the calabash, the earth upheaved of the tawny beast at the place engulfed beneath the floods; it is he, the master of the upheaved earth, of the swollen earth, beyond measure, he is the master of the basin of the earth.' The really interesting part of Brasseur's theory comes next, for he thought that, with the help of Landa's alphabet, he had identified the name of his ancient land: Mu. The land of Mu, as you will see in Chapter 4, is sometimes regarded by the 'experts' as another name for Atlantis itself, and sometimes as the name of its ghostly twin located in the Pacific.

4

THE UBIQUITOUS ATLANTEANS

ATLANTIS DORMANT

Interest in Atlantis waned somewhat after the European colonisation of the Americas, although there were always those who continued to speculate about its where-abouts. As I mentioned in Chapter 3, some explanation had to be found for the native population of the Americas. For people brought up in a Eurocentric society whose terms of reference were largely circumscribed by biblical teachings, the existence of other races could only be explained by recourse to the old idea of Noah's three sons – Shem, Ham and Japhet. Japhet was thought to be the father of all white Europeans, Ham of the black Africans and Shem of the Semitic race. Since the native Americans were clearly not European or African, they had to be Semitic. Then it was remembered that ten tribes of Jews had become 'lost' during the Exile in Babylon;

somehow they had made their way to the Americas where their descendants had lived ever since.

Variations on this theme suggested that the Egyptians, Phoenicians, or even the Assyrians were the progenitors of the native tribes. In many cases, their presence in the Americas was explained by means of Atlantis – America was either Atlantis itself or they must have used it as a stepping-stone en route as they travelled from the Middle East. Even more extraordinary was the belief that they were descendants of the Prince Madoc and his band of Welshmen who are supposed to have crossed the Atlantic in 1170. However, overall interest in the vexed location of Atlantis was fairly low until the 19th century.

VICTORIAN CONFIDENCE

In the Victorian society of the late 19th century, Atlantis truly resurfaced in the popular imagination, once again through a string of ambitious theories. Though many of these theories may seem quite eccentric today the intellectual climate of that particular period must be taken into consideration in order to understand how they were produced.

There was an unprecedented leap in all areas of science and technology between the 1860s and 1900. It was an age of great confidence, when most people thought science would provide all the answers to previously unsolved problems and mysteries. It was also the age of cataloguing and describing, when everything could be neatly fitted into some taxonomical system, whether plant, animal or human. Darwin had recently published his theories on evolution that either deeply fascinated or repelled his audience. It was a time when there was great interest in archaeology, especially Near Eastern archaeology, in the hope that the truths of the Bible would be proven conclusively.

With the discovery of the Assyrian and Babylonian civilisations, the deciphering of the forgotten languages of the region, and a growing awareness of the Asian languages and cultures of India, China and Japan, Europeans came to see that the history of the world was a great deal more complex than the Bible had suggested. Ease of access to the great libraries in the capitals of Europe and America made this the era of the 'self-taught scholar' – men and sometimes women with enquiring minds who lacked any formal education or training but who made up for this by voracious reading and the acquisition of 'facts'. A prime example of such a scholar was Ignatius Donnelly, the most influential and successful Atlantean theorist of all time, apart from Plato himself.

Ignatius Donnelly

Born in Philadelphia, Donnelly (1831–1901) was a restless and tirelessly active person who, like so many of his contemporaries, was fired-up with self-confidence and enthusiasm. Though undoubtedly a very talented and clever man, it was unfortunate that a lack of any formal discipline in his chosen area of study resulted in a conspicuous lack of critical sense, while over-confidence in his intellectual abilities led to many of his opinions being formed hastily. The same can also be said of his modern descendants, with their particular theories about the ancient world and the transmission of civilisation.

Earlier in his life, Donnelly had studied and practised law in the city of his birth but he later moved away with his family to a small rural town in Minnesota where he started publishing a local newspaper. He soon made a name for himself as the sophisticated and talented Easterner, for he was elected Lieutenant-Governor of Minnesota at the tender age of 28. He later went on to sit in the House of Representatives for eight years, although it seems that he spent most of his time reading enthusiastically in the Library of Congress rather than taking care of his electors' affairs.

Finally turned out of office in 1882, the fruits of his researches were published in his enormously successful book *Atlantis: The Antediluvian World*, which has since gone through more than 60 reprints. This was followed by *Ragnarok, The Age of Fire and Ice*, in which he argued that the last great Ice Age was brought to an end by a collision between the earth and a comet. Donnelly then turned his attention in a similarly authoritative manner to the mooted question of the identity of the author of Shakespeare's plays. Obviously a simple countryman become actor could not have written these works, so it must have been somebody of greater education and influence. He revealed all in *The Great Cryptogram*, which demonstrates that the true author was none other than Sir Francis Bacon. His fame grew exponentially and he continued to publish and travel on lecture tours for the rest of his life. Such was his prestige that he also became State Senator for Minnesota and ultimately ran, but failed to be elected, as Vice-President for the Populist party.

Donnelly's Atlantis

Through his wide-ranging studies in Washington, he read about the theories of certain other Atlantean writers. In particular, he was impressed by a young student named Edward Thompson, an undergraduate at the Worcester Polytechnic Institute. Thompson had published an article in *The Popular Science Monthly* that asserted that refugees from the sinking Atlantis had landed in North America, and then spread to Lake Superior. From there they were forced by hostile tribes to move on and migrate south to the Yucatan peninsular where their descendants created the Mayan culture. Ironically, Edward Thompson later repudiated these ideas and went on to become a respectable archaeologist specialising in the Mayan area.

In his *Atlantis: The Antediluvian World*, Donnelly set out to prove 'that there once existed in the Atlantic Ocean, opposite the mouth of the Mediterranean Sea, a large island, which was the remnant of an Atlantic continent, and known to the ancient world as Atlantis'. This basic premise is followed by a table of twelve secondary premises:

(1) That the description of this island given by Plato is not, as has long been supposed, fable, but veritable history.

(2) That Atlantis was the region where man first arose from a state of barbarism to civilisation.

(3) That it became, in the course of ages, a populous and mighty nation, from whose overflowings the shores of the Gulf of Mexico, the Mississippi River, the Amazon, the Pacific coast of South America, the Mediterranean, the west coast of Europe and Africa, the Baltic, the Black Sea, and the Caspian were populated by civilised nations.

(4) That it was the true Antediluvian world; the Garden of Eden; the Gardens of the Hesperides; the Elysian Fields; the Gardens of Alcinous; the Mesomphalos; the Olympos; the Asgard of the traditions of the ancient nations; representing a universal memory of a great land, where early mankind dwelt for ages in peace and happiness.

(5) That the gods and goddesses of the ancient Greeks, the Phoenicians, the Hindoos, and the Scandinavian were simply the kings, queens, and heroes of Atlantis; and the acts attributed to them in mythology are a confused recollection of real historical events.

(6) That the mythology of Egypt and Peru represented the original religion of Atlantis, which was sun worship.

(7) That the oldest colony formed by the Atlanteans was probably in Egypt, whose civilisation was a reproduction of that of the Atlantic island.

(8) That the implements of the 'Bronze Age' of Europe were derived from Atlantis. The Atlanteans were also the first manufacturers of iron.

(9) That the Phoenician alphabet, parent of all the European alphabets, was derived from an Atlantis alphabet, which was also conveyed from Atlantis to the Mayas of Central America.

(10) That Atlantis was the original seat of the Aryan or Indo-European family of nations, as well as the Semitic peoples, and possibly also of the Turanian races.

(11) That Atlantis perished in a terrible convulsion of nature, in which the whole island sunk into the ocean, with nearly all its inhabitants.

(12) That a few persons escaped in ships and on rafts, and carried to the nations east and west tidings of the appalling catastrophe, which has survived to our own time in the Flood and Deluge legends of different nations of the old and new worlds.

Diffusionism

Thus Donnelly laid out his basic hypotheses in a clear

and scientific manner, each of which he then proved in the remainder of his book. To the average non-specialist reader, this manner of presentation and wealth of apparently corroborative evidence seems overwhelming; Donnelly must have finally solved the enigma of Atlantis. However, only point 11 is actually derived from Plato's account. Nowhere does Plato say that the Atlanteans were the progenitors of world civilisation, or that there were any survivors who carried their knowledge to other parts of the world. In fact, a careful reading of the entire story reveals that the Atlanteans were portrayed as the villains of the piece and the truly civilised nation was that of the ancient Athenians. Yet Donnelly's theories were tremendously influential and have been inherited in modified form by many writers since, most notably by Graham Hancock.

The idea that all major cultural developments in the world derive from a single source is known as the diffusionist theory. Thus, for example, writing was not invented independently and at different times in the Middle East, China and South America, but derives from one single invention which was transmitted throughout the world by some means. Similarly, the fact that there are pyramids in Egypt and South America must point to a common source – despite the clear differences in construction, purpose and age. One could continue, as Donnelly did, with an explanation for the origin of all human achievements in this manner.

Atlantis in the Atlantic

In Chapter 2 I explained that part of Plato's technique in creating the apparent authenticity of a story was to write a pastiche in the style of the 'new historians' like Thucydides, who demanded detail and accuracy without fantastic embellishments. Donnelly overlooked this factor, for he maintained that the lack of magical or fantastic elements in the account of Atlantis proved that Plato's story was true. Because he believed in the literal truth of the Atlantis story, he had to find its location and account for its demise. Seizing upon the information that had just come to light with the first oceanographic survey of the Atlantic, Donnelly saw evidence of a sunken Atlantis in a band of submarine mountains known as the Mid-Atlantic Ridge, up to a thousand metres below the surface, as well as the mountainous islands such as the Azores and the Canaries. Moreover, to complete the picture, Donnelly believed that Atlantis was connected to the Old and New Worlds by several other submerged land ridges. Unfortunately, marine geologists have since found that there could never have been a large land mass in that location. The Mid-Atlantic Ridge is actually the result of movement in the tectonic plates at that point, where they are drifting apart with deep fissures opening which continually release lava that has accumulated and formed underwater mountains.

Since Donnelly's Atlantis was many hundreds of fathoms below the surface, he had to account for its

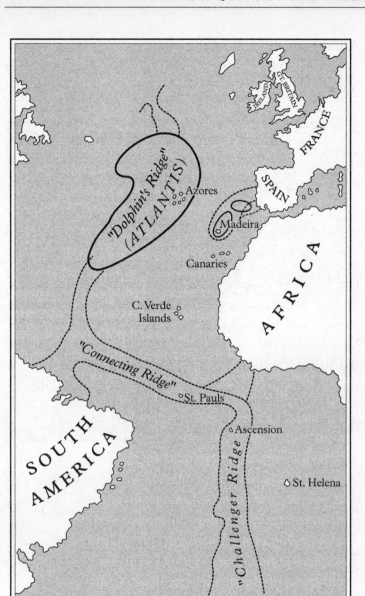

A map of Atlantis according to Ignatias Donnelly *(1882)*

submergence. Once again, science came to his rescue. Donnelly had heard that continents had risen and fallen thousands of feet during geological ages and knew that indeed some islands had also risen or sunk in a matter of hours during volcanic eruptions. If that was the case, why could not the whole continent of Atlantis have sunk as a result of earthquakes or volcanic eruption? Hence, he came to the conclusion that 'it is proven beyond question, by geological evidence, that vast masses of land once existed in the region where Plato located Atlantis, and therefore such an island must have existed; ... that there is nothing improbable or impossible in the statement that it was destroyed by an earthquake in one dreadful night and day'.

Cultural Parallels

To further strengthen his case, Donnelly pointed out chance resemblances between various species of American and European flora and fauna. He tried to prove using a range of often dubious authorities, that plants such as tobacco, pineapples or cotton were not confined to one continent before Columbus as was generally thought, but were grown in both Old and New Worlds. Thus he saw pineapples in Assyrian reliefs, which were actually date-palms! Similarly, he advocated strong diffusionist theories concerning pyramids, burial-mounds, metallurgy, the arts, agriculture, ships; they all originated in his Atlantis and spread to the neighbouring areas, for he could not conceive that human genius had duplicated many inventions throughout the world.

To some degree, his enthusiasm is understandable. At the time when he was writing, many of the dating techniques such as Carbon 14 were unavailable and scientific archaeology was still in its infancy. What was known about early Egyptian civilisation was incomplete for it seemed to many that the characteristic culture of the Nile Valley had blossomed all at once without slow evolution. To Donnelly, this showed that it had to have been imported from outside.

Language and Myth

Though no linguist himself, Donnelly tried to prove that similar alphabets existed on both sides of the Atlantic. He took the Mayan 'alphabet' concocted by Landa in the 16th century, and by extracting and distorting elements of the Mayan glyphs, claimed that the script was originally identical to that used by the Phoenicians of the ancient Mediterranean world. His interest in the Mayan language did not end there. Conveniently for Donnelly, there was another individual working in the field, Augustus le Plongeon, who developed his own Atlantean theories. Taking him as a reliable source, Donnelly quoted le Plongeon's confident words that 'one third of the Mayan tongue is pure Greek'. He also mentioned a certain Melgor of Mexico who said that the Central American language, Chiapanec, closely resembled Hebrew. Similarly, he picked up on the idea that the Otomi language of Mexico is related to Chinese – in this case, probably because they use tones to distinguish words.

Like Euhemerus in ancient times, Donnelly assumed that most myths are merely distortions of actual historical events. That being the case, it was not difficult for Donnelly to reconstruct a detailed history of Atlantis by assuming that all Old World myths in the book of Genesis are distorted accounts of Atlantean history. According to Donnelly, all the gods of the Old World were really Atlantean kings, queens or other famous people. It also took no great leap of imagination to see a common theme and source in the abundance of flood myths around the world, many of which had been collected by Donnelly's time. They too are nothing more than distorted accounts of the great catastrophe that befell his Atlantis in the Atlantic.

Augustus le Plongeon

The illustrious French physician Augustus le Plongeon (1826–1908) was the first European to excavate Mayan ruins in Yucatan. He cuts a somewhat pathetic figure, for despite his genuine familiarity with the language and custom of the Maya, his work failed to achieve scientific recognition despite having battled for many years against the Yucatan jungle and corrupt Mexican officials. The first fruits of his labours were contained in an introductory book called *Sacred Mysteries Among the Maya and Quiches*

11,500 Years Ago (1886), but this was predictably scorned by serious scholars. He followed this with his extensive volume *Queen Moo and the Egyptian Sphinx*. Like many other ardent diffusionists, he was unhappy that the scholarly establishment had derided and rejected his cherished life work, and he thoroughly denounced the 'arrogance and self-conceit of superficial learning' displayed by the 'pretended authorities'.

It is in *Queen Moo and the Egyptian Sphinx* that the florid fantasy of le Plongeon's Atlantis is encountered in detail. His account of Atlantis uses Brasseur's version of the *Codex Troano* and some inscriptions on the walls of Chichen-Itza to create a romantic story about the rivalry between the princes Coh and Aac for the hand of their sister Moo, the queen of Atlantis or Mu. Coh won but was murdered by Aac who conquered the country and seized it from Moo. Then disaster befell the land. As the continent sank below the waves, Moo fled with the body of Coh to Egypt. There she became known as Isis while her dead brother was none other than the god Osiris in whose memory she built the Sphinx. Meanwhile, other survivors from Mu-Atlantis settled in Central America where they became the Maya.

Though no such story exists in Mayan mythology, many students of Atlantis still quote le Plongeon's imaginative story as fact to corroborate the existence of Atlantis. Mu, on the other hand, has taken on an independent life of its own in the work of James Churchward, as we shall see shortly.

Paul Schliemann

Another important figure in the modern history of Atlantis is Dr Paul Schliemann, the grandson of the famous Heinrich Schliemann, renowned as the discoverer and excavator of Troy and Mycenae. Feeling somewhat left in the shadows by the fame of his illustrious grandfather, Paul Schliemann published an article in the *New York American* in 1912 called 'How I Discovered Atlantis, the Source of All Civilization'. In it, he claimed that his grandfather had left him an envelope of papers on archaeological matters and an ancient owl-headed vase. The envelope bore a warning in his grandfather's handwriting that it should only be opened by a member of the family who was willing to devote the rest of his life to investigating the matters contained therein. Schliemann vowed to do so and opened the envelope. The first instructions were to break open the vase, which he did, and inside found some square coins made of a curious alloy of platinum, aluminium and silver, as well as a metal plate with the words 'Issued in the Temple of the Transparent Walls' inscribed upon it in Phoenician. In his grandfather's notes, he claimed to have found an account of the discovery of a large bronze jar at Troy. In this jar were coins and artefacts of metal, bone and pottery. Both the jar and some of the other objects bore the inscription 'From King Kronos of Atlantis'.

Paul Schliemann went on to use the same diffusionist arguments for the existence of Atlantis as had Donnelly and le Plongeon. He claimed to know of the account recorded in the *Codex Troano* about the sinking of Mu – which he said he had read in the British Museum, though it was actually kept in Madrid – and that by chance he had found this record of events corroborated in a mysterious 4,000-year-old Chaldean manuscript kept in the Tibetan capital, Lhasa. The Chaldean account told of the destruction of the Land of the Seven Cities by earthquakes and eruptions after the star Bel fell. Though Schliemann promised his eager public that he would reveal all in a book, sadly he never did so, nor did anybody get to see the strange coins or the jar which contained them.

James Churchward and Mu

The true soul-mate of Donnelly must be the Anglo-American James Churchward. Like Donnelly, he was a largely self-educated man with a vivid imagination, though slightly dubious credentials. He claimed to have travelled widely in Asia and Central America during his earlier years, though the truth of this has not been ascertained independently. He also awarded himself the honorary title of 'colonel' to give himself panache in later life. His first publication did not appear until he was quite old; *The Lost Continent of Mu* was published in 1926, soon to be followed by others. He too had his own distinctive hypotheses about Atlantis and its companion continent, Mu, in the Pacific. Like others before and after him, his

ideas are primarily based on the discredited theories of le
Plongeon and Paul Schliemann.

With Churchward, we encounter a heady blend of
occult dogmas and secret documents. A central element
of his researches is based on the esoteric significance of
certain common symbols found throughout the world.
Typically, he claims that a rectangle is actually the
Muvian sign for 'Mu' – since rectangles can be found
everywhere, this proves the pervasiveness of Muvian
culture. Less thorough in some respects than Donnelly,
his book is full of palpable fictions and distortions such as
his amended version of Plato, whom Churchward quotes
as stating that 'the land of Mu had ten peoples'.

Most important in his discovery of Mu are two sets of
inscribed tablets that he claims to have seen and deciphered. One set of these tablets was apparently found in
Mexico and formed part of a private American collection
when Churchward found them. He reproduces illustra-
tions of these 'tablets', which to the uninitiated look like
nothing more than the very common flattened Aztec
clay figurines with engraved decorations. However,
Churchward believed they were tablets with esoteric
Muvian inscriptions which he was able to interpret.

The other set of tablets is even more bizarre. He
refers to them as the 'Naacal tablets', which bear writings in Naga symbols and characters. The Nagas are
actually mythological Indian serpents and the name of a
group of tribal people living in north-eastern India.
Nevertheless, Churchward claims that he was shown

these tablets by a kind priest in India or in Tibet, and that he could immediately read them because they were written in an ancient language which he had, coincidentally, just been studying.

In these tablets, he read an account of the creation of the world and of the submergence of Mu. He also learnt that Mu was a large Pacific continent which stretched over a vast area from the Hawaiian islands to Fiji and from the Easter Islands to the Marianas, and that the inhabitants of Mu had an advanced civilisation which contributed many major cultural and technological advances to the rest of humanity. In its heyday, Mu apparently had a population of sixty-four million inhabitants who were divided into ten tribes, with a philosopher-king called Ra ruling over them. In Churchward's account of Mu can also be found the unpleasant tinges of racism that were often linked to Atlantean theories. Thus, although the skins of the Muvians were of several hues, those with white skin dominated them all. As would be expected, the Muvians also practised the pure Aryan monotheism which Jesus later tried to revive in Israel.

In its humanitarian ventures, Mu sent out colonists under the guidance of its priests, the Naacal. Some of these colonists went to Atlantis and then went on to occupy the Amazon basin, while others settled in Asia and built a Uighur Empire. But then disaster struck. Some 15,000 years ago, the 'gas-belts' – gas-filled caves which lay under much of the earth – collapsed and both Mu and Atlantis sank below the waves. The thousands of Muvian survivors were left trapped upon crowded Polynesian islands with insufficient food to feed themselves. In their desperation, they resorted to cannibalism and thus fell to primitive savagery.

Blavatsky and Lemuria

Though many Atlantean and Muvian theories may seem far-fetched to people today, the occult Atlantean world of Blavatsky and her followers took things into another dimension.

Helena Blavatsky (1831–1891) was born in old Tsarist Russia. Again, in her case, authentic details of her earlier life are hard to come by since she found it necessary to reinvent herself in a manner more appropriate to her role in the occult world. However, from what is known she led an extremely colourful life. She was, in turn, the wife of a Russian general, the mistress of a Slovenian singer, of an English businessman, of a Russian baron, and many others. Her professional life was equally varied – she worked as a circus bareback rider, a professional pianist, a businesswoman and a spiritualist medium. Somewhere on her travels she picked up a good working knowledge of the Western occult and magic traditions as well as a wide but superficial knowledge of Eastern philosophy and myths.

While living in New York as an émigrée during the 1870s, she formed a relationship with a lawyer, Henry Steel Olcott, who left his wife and children to be with her. In 1875 they founded the Theosophical Society and soon afterwards moved to India together to search for higher knowledge. While there, she claims she began to receive letters from her spirit master Koot Hoomi, though subsequent graphological analysis has shown that they were in her own handwriting. Regardless of her explanation of the source of the letters, their contents became increasingly convoluted and gradually elaborated a bizarre occult cosmology.

She eventually put together all these teachings into a vast book called *The Secret Doctrine*. This was supposedly based on a mysterious ancient manuscript known as the *Book of Dzyan* preserved in Tibet, although no such book is known to scholars. She claimed that she had been shown this book by the Mahatmas, a group of highly advanced spiritual beings who resided in Tibet and guided the world through their occult energy. In fact, it was clearly demonstrated by William Coleman and others that she had merely plagiarised passages from the *Rig Veda*, the *Vishnu Purana*, Donnelly's *Atlantis* and other contemporary works.

Blavatsky had heard of Atlantis and Lemuria and soon incorporated them into her cosmology. Atlantis is a familiar name, but Lemuria may not have much resonance for people today. The concept started as a respectable scientific hypothesis, reasonable in its day. It had been noted in the 1870s that there were similar fossils at the same strata level in India, Madagascar and Africa, so scientists were led to hypothesise on the existence of an Indo-Madagascan land-bridge which they called Gondwana. Soon after, the German palaeontologist Ernst Hackel, a keen advocate of Darwinian theories of evolution, seized on this idea of a land-bridge to explain the presence of lemurs in Madagascar, India, Africa and Malaysia. Hence the name Lemuria. In addition, since this land-bridge must have existed during the Cenozoic Age, as lemurs were both mammals and monkeys, then perhaps this area might also have been the original home of humans who in crude Darwinian terms were descended from the same ancestors as simians and the great apes.

This Lemurian land-bridge theory has now been discarded with the discovery of tectonic plates and continental drift. Occultists, on the other hand, have retained the notion of Lemuria and sometimes transfer its location to the Pacific and use it as a synonym for the lost continent of Mu.

It is well beyond the scope of this book to give all the details of Blavatsky's occult cosmology, as taught by her and enlarged by her followers Sinnet and Besant, but some salient points can be usefully summarised here, though it should be noted that none of the ideas have any archaeological corroboration. Blavatsky believed that there were a total of seven Root Races, each of which were divided into seven sub-races. Working forwards from the distant past and the first glimmer of material life, to the present day, five of these Root Races have come into being. The first consisted of invisible astral beings

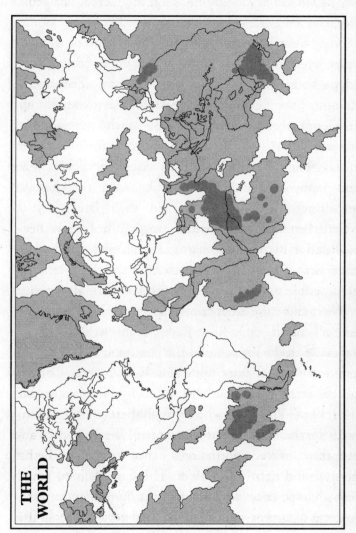

Lemuria according to the Theosophists. The shaded areas depict the extent of Lemuria, while darker areas represent mountainous regions. (*After Scott-Elliot*)

who lived in the Imperishable Sacred Land, sometimes called Polarea. They did not have any sexual differentiation but reproduced by fission, rather like amoebas.

They were followed by slightly more substantial beings who lived in Arctic Hyperborea. Later, the land of Hyperborea broke up and led to the formation of Lemuria. The Lemurians are described as somewhat ape-like hermaphroditic egg-laying giants who were additionally blessed with four arms and an eye on the back of their heads. Their downfall was their discovery of sex. When this happened, the divine beings known as the Lhas were so disgusted that they turned their backs on the Lemurians who were instead taught the basic skills of civilisation by advanced beings from Venus. It is said that their descendants are still present in the world as 'primitive' people such as the Lapps and the Aborigines.

Next came the Atlanteans, the fourth Root Race who, like all the previous Root Races, comprised several sub-races. With the break-up of the continent of Lemuria, the continent of Atlantis miraculously appeared. This was colonised along its southern shores by the black-skinned 12-foot tall Rmoahals who through their constant conflict with survivors of Lemuria invented warfare and murder. As they moved northwards, they gradually became shorter and lighter in colour. The Cro-Magnon people, known to science, were their direct descendants.

Next to appear were a red-skinned group, the Tlavatlis, who originated on an island to the west of Atlantis. They migrated into the mountain regions of Atlantis and then

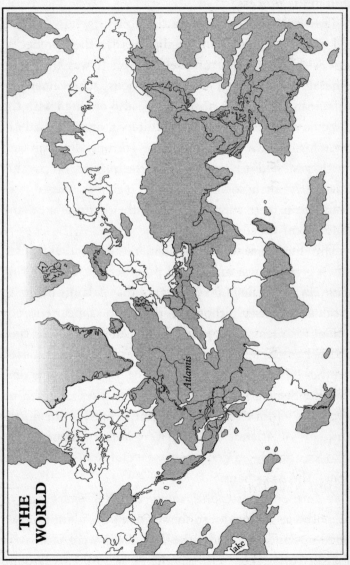

THE
WORLD

Atlantis

lake

Atlantis according to the Theosophists – Atlantis lies in the area of the Atlantic Ocean, while Lemuria covers much of Asia and Austronesia. (*After Scott-Elliot*)

took over from the backward Rmoahals, inventing king-ship in the process.

Then came the sub-race of the Toltecs, who were also red-skinned although a little shorter than their predecessors with a height of only eight feet. It was they who ushered in a golden age of glorious achievement in Atlantean civilisation, and they are also credited with the discovery of the concept of hereditary monarchy. Later in their history, the Toltecs became corrupt, arrogant and much addicted to sorcery and the misuse of psychic powers. As their society began to teeter on the edge of destruction, the Turanians made their appearance and finished off the Toltecs.

The Turanians were cruel and ruthless individualists, much given to war and sexual promiscuity. It was during their era, some 800,000 years ago, that Atlantis began to break up and sink, although it did not disappear entirely. Some Turanians escaped to South America where they became the Aztecs while others went to Asia and started another sub-race, the Mongolians. It was also at this time that the Semite and the Akkadian sub-races emerged on what was left of Atlantis. The Semites lived in the northern parts of Atlantis but they were a quarrelsome nation who constantly raided their peaceful southern neighbours, the Akkadians.

A further catastrophe some 200,000 years ago is supposed to have reduced the remnants of Atlantis to two smaller islands. Happily, the Akkadians were ultimately able to drive out the Semites from Atlantis around

100,000 years ago. Around this time, Akkadian colonists also settled in the Middle East where they developed their legal and mercantile skills. Then the smaller southern island of Atlantis disappeared under the waves, while the larger northern island was reduced further in size around 80,000 years ago. What was left of Atlantis finally submerged forever around 10,000 years ago and it was this portion of Atlantis that is described by Plato in his works.

Subsequently, the modern Root Race of Aryans developed from selected Semites who were seen to constitute 'an abnormal and unnatural link between the Fourth and Fifth Root Races'. This incipient yet fashionable racism was to bear a tragic fruit in the 20th century with the rise of the Nazis.

The Nazis and Atlantis

There was a secret organisation with its headquarters in Munich called the Thule Society (*Thule Gesellschaft*). It derived its name from the legendary island in the North Sea that was believed to be a part of Atlantis and to have served as a refuge for the fleeing Atlantean Aryans; as such it was seen as the source of all higher culture.

Dedicated to occultism and the establishment of a pan-German state, the Thule Society set up and funded the German Workers Party with the specific aims of promoting German nationalism, anti-Communism, anti-Semitism and the supremacy of the Aryan race. Adolf Hitler joined the German Workers Party after the First World War and soon took over its leadership, transforming it into the National Socialist Party. The notion of an Aryan 'master race' appealed to Hitler and he quickly adopted many of its ideas in his bid to create a German super-state. He also seems to have believed that Aryans originated in Atlantis and that it was his destiny to restore the Aryan race to its original pristine purity. Heinrich Himmler, who became head of the SS, was also especially interested in the occult and tried to make his contribution to civilisation by eliminating the various 'inferior races', thus unleashing the Holocaust that destroyed the lives of over six million men, women and children.

It is a tragic irony that this 20th-century nightmare should have derived, albeit in a very distorted manner, from the Atlantis teachings of Plato who had wanted to create an ideal city-state free from brutality and injustice.

5

ATLANTIS IN THE MEDITERRANEAN

SALVAGING THE ATLANTIS MYTH

After the end of the 19th century, great strides were made in our understanding of the earth's geological history. With the development and general acceptance of the theory of continental drift and tectonic plates, it became clear that the existence of a lost, sunken continent either in the Atlantic or the Pacific was quite improbable. Previous theories about mysterious land-bridges were also no longer necessary to explain similarities in the flora and fauna of neighbouring continents.

Furthermore, considerable advances in our knowledge of human prehistory made through a combination of archaeology and linguistics seriously compromised the position of the early diffusionist theories. Advanced dating techniques such as Carbon 14 and dendrochronology have resulted in important new findings about the development of agriculture, metal-working and urban settlement. It is now known that the earliest substantial Neolithic settlements did not develop until 8000 BCE at the earliest, while metal-working – beginning with the use of copper – only began around 3000 BCE. The use of iron came much later, with very different starting dates around the world; the earliest samples were probably found no earlier than 1500 BCE. The wide variation in dates for the introduction of all these technological advances undermines the classical Atlantean diffusionist theories since one would expect them to be largely contemporary in the regions where settled cultures developed in South East Asia, China, Japan, the Middle East and South America.

In the wake of these discoveries, some scholars have tried to salvage something of Plato's Atlantis myth. Since the earlier grandiose explanations have been discredited, several more rational albeit modest theories have been put forward in recent years. It is characteristic of these theories that they all maintain a belief in the veracity of Plato's account but recognise that various elements of the story may be distorted or exaggerated. Since Plato says that the account is true, then either it did originate in Egypt or else Plato constructed it from scraps of knowledge about earlier cultures in the Greek world that were still available in his time. Whatever the case, a compromise must be made between the account and the archaeological facts and hence certain elements must be disregarded or modified, especially regarding the dating and linear measurements mentioned in Plato's account. The easiest solution to adopt is that Plato did not necessarily receive his very detailed account of Atlantis from Egypt via Solon as he would have us believe, but put together a number of elements derived from various sources, all relating to cities or nations that were located in the Mediterranean. This view is appealing as there are a number of suitable candidates who could have served Plato's purpose, while there are inherent difficulties in maintaining the Egyptian connection.

ANCIENT SEAFARERS

During the 20th century, several attempts were made to identify Atlantis with places that would have been within the Greek cultural horizon. In the present day, when we have access to most parts of the world, it is easy for us to forget that this was not always the case. Remember that the type of ships available to people in the ancient world were generally extremely flimsy, easily sunk in storms even in the relative calm of the Mediterranean let alone out in the waters of the Atlantic. Navigational skills were usually poor so ships would sail close to the shores, within sight of land.

For people living around the coasts of the Mediterranean in ancient times, it took many centuries for their horizons to be extended, by even a relatively short distance, and some cultures showed very little interest in lands overseas. The Egyptians, for example, generally seem to have been quite uninterested in maritime explorations, apart from the famous journey to the fabled land of Punt on the African coast sponsored by Queen Hatshepsut in the 14th century BCE. Indeed, Plato's account of an Egyptian custom of keeping records of important overseas events is quite at odds with the facts. Judging from the bulk of surviving material, Egyptian society was fairly introverted and xenophobic for most of her history, apart from a flurry of diplomatic correspondence from the period just prior to Tutankhamun in the 12th century BCE. The idea that the Egyptians had somehow kept a detailed account of something like Atlantis for thousands of years, and moreover had carved it on a column in Sais, seems fairly implausible. They did have a degree of contact with the outside Mediterranean world, but most incoming ships at Egyptian ports would have belonged to other more capable seafarers such as the Minoans, whom they knew as the Kheftiu, and later the Phoenicians.

The Minoans seem to have functioned as seafaring traders for several hundred years until the collapse and destruction of their culture sometime around the 15th century BCE. I shall return to the Minoans later since there are some who would link them with the Atlantis myth.

GREEK KNOWLEDGE OF THE MEDITERRANEAN

It is clear that Greek knowledge of the Mediterranean was also limited for many centuries judging from information contained in the *Iliad* and *Odyssey*, attributed to Homer but not actually dating from much earlier than the 7th century BCE. On stylistic grounds, it is generally recognised that they cannot even be from the same hand but would have been composed at different periods of Greek history, the *Iliad* being the earlier of the two. In as far as places can be identified with certainty, the Greeks of that period were only familiar with the eastern end of the Mediterranean to southern Italy and Sicily. By the time of Solon (c.640–560 BCE), the supposed recipient of the Atlantis story, the Greeks knew of the coastal areas of the lands bordering the Mediterranean and somewhat more of the Middle East, as far away as Babylon on the Euphrates, although much of this knowledge was still second-hand from other nations.

It should also be mentioned here that the use of the word 'Atlantic' in Plato's account of the Great Sea, which the Greeks believed surrounded the known world, is anachronistic if the story of Atlantis truly derives from Solon. The first use of the name 'Atlantic' in reference to what we call the Atlantic Ocean occurs in Herodotus' *History*, over 100 years after Solon's death. Though it derives from the mountainous area where the giant Atlas was thought to live, the Greeks knew of several places purporting to be his residence, including North Africa, Turkey, Crete and Ethiopia. Moreover, it did not always refer to the Atlantic Ocean, for even as late as the 3rd century some writers applied the name to the Indian Ocean. It is therefore even less likely that the original Egyptian source, if such existed, would have used the name, because such distant regions lay well beyond the sphere of Egyptian knowledge and interest.

The extent of the world known to Greeks at the time of Plato, according to the geographer Hekataios. (*After Bunbury*)

In Plato's time, this knowledge had extended further eastwards towards India but hardly further than southern Spain to the west. The difficulty for the Greeks, even had they wanted to travel to the western end of the Mediterranean, was the presence of the important trading empire of the Phoenicians based at Carthage in present-day Tunisia. The Phoenicians jealously guarded their trading monopoly throughout that region and actively discouraged stray Greek and later Roman ships from entering those waters. It seems that the Phoenicians were the greatest sailors in the Mediterranean for centuries, and it is believed that they made journeys of considerable distance along the African coast at least as far as the Canary Isles. Until the later Roman period, the Phoenicians were the only ancient people to venture beyond the Mediterranean into the Atlantic.

TARTESSOS

When we look closer to home for the location of a city or civilisation which may have provided material for Plato's account of Atlantis, there are several possible candidates. As I mentioned above, it is always necessary in such cases to abandon the dating given by Plato, who said that the Atlantean and ancient Athenian cultures flourished more than 9,000 years before his time. Scholars either completely disregard the dating or reduce it by about a factor of ten to bring it into line with Mediterranean dates which are known archaeologically – that is, Plato's account is interpreted as referring to a period around 950 BCE rather than 9,500 BCE.

The phrase 'the Pillars of Heracles', in its later popular sense, refers to the Straits of Gibraltar. Just beyond the Straits on the banks of the River Guadalquivir near to present-day Cadiz, a site was discovered and partially excavated in the 1920s by Professor Adolf Schulten. He believed he had found the fabled city of Tartessos which was located in the area. Schulten believed that the city gave rise to the Atlantis myth.

Tartessos was so famous for its wealth and seafaring merchants that its existence was known even to biblical writers such as Isaiah and Ezekiel who called it 'Tarshish'. Little is known of the history of this city, or the identity of its inhabitants who could have been Iberian natives, Phoenician or Etruscan settlers, though it may never be known for certain. Certainly they had extensive mercantile links with the Phoenicians at the eastern end of the Mediterranean. Around 1000 BCE they are known to have traded huge amounts of silver mined locally for olive oil – silver was so common that the Phoenicians are said to have cast their anchor-stones from Tartessian silver in order to carry away as much as possible.

King Hiram of the Phoenician city of Tyre formed a trading alliance with King Solomon, sending their trading fleets to trade with Tartessos every three years. They are said to have returned with gold, silver, ivory, peacocks and apes. When Tyre fell, the prophet Ezekiel wrote,

'Tarshish was thy merchant by reason of the multitude of all kinds of riches; with silver, iron, tin and lead they traded in thy fairs'.

The Greeks are said to have first made direct contact with Tartessos in 631 BCE when a Samian ship bound for Egypt was blown miles off course and put into Tartessos. The detour seems to have been worthwhile, for the crew are said to have made their fortunes in the trade goods they brought back. A little later, the Phokaians from Ionia commenced trading with Tartessos on a regular basis, ever wary of the predatory Carthaginian warships guarding their home waters.

With the development of trade, the Greeks incorporated this end of the Mediterranean world into their mythology. The hero Heracles, whose legends were themselves of Phoenician origin, is said to have stopped over at Tartessos. So the story goes, Heracles borrowed a magical golden cup from the sun god and used it to perform one of his legendary tasks. At the same time, it is said that he erected two pillars at the Straits of Gibraltar, but it is unclear whether this is the same set of pillars that he erected at the abode of Atlas.

Thus, though little is known about Tartessos, its wealth was legendary and it is quite likely that some accounts of the city would have been known to Plato and used by him as contributory material for his Atlantis story. The last known report of Tartessos was around 500 BCE, for it was probably destroyed around that time by the Carthaginian general Himilco in order to eliminate competition with the neighbouring but rival Phoenician city of Gades. It is also known that the Carthaginians deliberately created scare stories to discourage traders from other nations venturing out past the Straits of Gibraltar. When Plato said that the Atlantic became impassable after the destruction of Atlantis due to silt, he may have been duped by the Phoenician policy of disinformation.

CARTHAGE

The powerful western Phoenician outpost of Carthage has also been suggested as a candidate in providing some of Plato's Atlantis material. Carthage was founded around 850 BCE by one Princess Elissa, known to the Romans as Dido. Due to its favourable location and the maritime skills of the Phoenicians, Carthage soon became a powerful state with a virtual monopoly of trade throughout that region, effectively blocking passage to all other nations. Their trading voyages took them as far afield as the British Isles to the north, from where they obtained tin, and to the coast of Africa for other exotic goods.

Not only were they obstructive to other traders, the Carthaginians were positively expansionist. Until the destruction of Carthage by the Romans in 146 BCE at the end of the Punic Wars, the Carthaginians set up colonies all around the western Mediterranean, from the Iberian peninsular across to parts of Sicily and southern Italy where they came into constant conflict with the

Greek colonies such as Syracuse and the emergent state of Rome. Indeed, the Carthaginians came within a hair's breadth of defeating Rome, with its brilliant generals such as Hannibal. How different world history would be today if Rome had been subjugated by the Carthaginians!

During his sojourn in Sicily, Plato would have become very familiar with the menace of the Carthaginians and some have thought that this lies behind his account of the arrogant and wealthy land of Atlantis that menaced all the lands around, as Plato says, 'they ruled over Libya as far as Egypt and over Europe as far as Tuscany'.

Excavations at Carthage have also revealed some parallels with the capital city of Atlantis as described by Plato. It had a walled citadel located upon a low hill on which also stood a temple, later said to be dedicated to Asclepius, the god of healing, rather than Poseidon, the god of the sea, which would have been more appropriate for the maritime Carthaginians. This citadel was strengthened by three huge ramparts that surrounded it. Nearer to the shore, a huge waterway had been constructed around a central island, leading in from the sea, with roofed docks arranged around it. A second, smaller canal led south into a commercial harbour used by Carthaginian traders. The land around Carthage was marshy but cut across with drainage canals and channels supplying fresh water. It is the overall circular pattern of Carthage that bears some resemblance to Plato's description of Atlantis. One wonders whether Plato might have heard details of the layout of Carthage while visiting

Sicily and incorporated its features, suitably exaggerated, into his account.

THE MINOAN CIVILISATION

One of the strongest candidates for the inspiration behind Plato's Atlantis story is the Cretan-based Minoan civilisation. This view is well argued by Rodney Castleden in his *Atlantis Destroyed*, in which he details over 80 specific parallels between the Minoan culture and Plato's account. The very existence of the Minoan culture had been lost in the mists of time until excavations on Crete and neighbouring islands began at the end of the 19th century, most notably through the efforts of Sir Arthur Evans. Since then much has been learnt about this great Bronze Age civilisation which once dominated the eastern Mediterranean.

It is now known that this culture flourished from about 2200 BCE until its abrupt demise around 1430 BCE. A number of splendid palace-like structures have been discovered on Crete at Knossos, Phaistos and Mallia, among other places. There is no unanimity of opinion among scholars as to whether these were palaces of independent city-states, or even whether they were palaces at all, but it is worth remembering that Plato recorded that the Atlanteans had a confederation of kings. The largest of the Minoan settlements was at Knossos, where a great sanctuary-cum-palace has been excavated. It is highly likely that this sanctuary was dedicated to Poseidon, the chief of the Minoan gods; this again tallies with Plato's account of the religious inclinations of the Atlanteans. It is also thought that this building was the origin of the Greek legend of the labyrinth, which housed a savage bull-headed man to whom the Greeks were obliged to send regular human sacrificial victims until it was slain by the Athenian hero Theseus. There is another point of similarity here between Plato's account of Atlantis and the Minoan culture. Plato outlines a religious ritual that involved bulls, while scholars believe from painted murals and other evidence that the Minoans followed similar practices.

During the period of their hegemony over the eastern Mediterranean, the Minoans were famed as a nation of seafaring traders backed up with considerable military power. They are known to have traded regularly with the Egyptians, and are mentioned several times in surviving inscriptions where they are referred to as Kheftiu. Like the Phoenicians, the Minoans seem to have had a stranglehold on trade in that part of the world, bringing goods from far and wide. They were also an expansionistic culture since their settlements have been found not only on Crete itself but on many surrounding islands, and traces have even been found on the Greek and Asian mainlands. Like the Carthaginians several hundred years after them, they seem to have been determined to maintain control over their monopoly, and probably resorted to various forms of intimidation against their weaker neighbours. The Greek legend of the labyrinth, mentioned above, may well be a distant memory of the tribute they were required to pay the Minoans.

The mainland of Greece was at this time inhabited by the Bronze Age Mycenaeans who had dominated the country from around 1600 BCE, with their chief centres at Mycenae (after which they take their name), Tiryns, Pylos and Athens. Sufficient knowledge of their later culture would have survived in legend down to Plato's time to serve as the model of his small but morally superior Athens which led a confederacy against the Atlanteans. Historically, we know that the Mycenaeans did invade and conquer the Minoan centres of settlement and established their rule over Crete and the other islands of the Aegean Sea.

The Minoans and Atlantis

In Plato's account of Atlantis, the sequence of events is as follows: the Atlanteans plan to conquer Greece but are defeated by the ancient Athenians. Just as they are defeated, a great cataclysm strikes and wipes out Atlantis as well as the Greek armies. Does this correspond in any way to known historical events? The answer must be yes, but not in that sequence. When Knossos and other Minoan sites were first excavated, it was immediately noticed that they had all suffered severe earthquake damage. And when Santorini, or Thera as it was once known, came to be excavated in the 1930s, it soon became apparent that this small island north of Crete had been totally devastated by an enormous volcanic eruption which had blown away almost two-thirds of the island. It was then understood that accompanying earthquakes and tsunami were the likely causes of the severe damage seen on Crete itself and elsewhere.

The precise dating of this event is controversial but the consensus is that it would have been sometime around 1530 BCE. Memories of the huge amount of damage caused by the eruption would have lasted for decades, if not centuries, in the neighbouring countries, including Greece and Egypt. The Minoan culture did not immediately collapse for some rebuilding is known to have taken place. Its power in the Mediterranean must have been severely weakened, however. One can assume that the Mycenaeans on the Greek mainland took advantage of this period of weakness and seized control of the Minoan territories.

It is also quite possible that during this period of geological instability there was some kind of further destruction which wiped out some of the Mycenaean forces, memories of which were incorporated as an extra ingredient into Plato's account of Atlantis. Again, if by chance Plato's story did originally come from Egypt as he says, then it must have seemed to them as if the Minoan civilisation had disappeared from the face of the earth, within the cessation of all contact with their erstwhile trading partners.

Textual Problems of Dating and Measurement

Rodney Castleden thinks it is feasible that details of the Minoan civilisation as Atlantis could have been transmitted to Plato via papers passed down in his family from the time of Solon. He makes a number of suggestions to account for the larger-than-life units of time and distance used by Plato, and considers the possibility that accounts of the destruction of the Minoan civilisation were written in the characteristic Minoan Linear A or B scripts by survivors of the disaster, possibly in Egypt itself. He notes that the symbol used for '100' is very similar to the one used for '1,000', the difference being the presence or absence of a few small ticks around a circle. However, as Castleden points out, how would these hypothetical Minoans have known that they were living 900 or even 9,000 years before Solon!

He also suggests that the error may have arisen through a scribal misreading of one of the cursive versions of Egyptian hieroglyphs known as hieratic and demotic. Alternatively, the problem could have arisen through a misunderstanding on the part of Solon regarding the calendrical method being used – the Egyptians used lunar cycles, each one being a mini-year, with a total of 12.3 per solar year. This would date the fall of Atlantis at around 1330 BCE, which does correspond to the end of the Minoan civilisation after the great volcanic eruption and earthquakes. However, it should be noted that there is still the problem of the huge dimensions given for the various features found in and around the capital of Atlantis.

Castleden also makes some interesting points regarding the location of Atlantis as described by Plato, and the realities of the Minoan culture based on Crete. One key problem that has caused so many Atlantis seekers to look to the Atlantic Ocean is the statement by Plato that Atlantis was larger than Asia and Libya combined. In the original Greek, the word for 'greater' is *'mezon'*, but there is also a similar word meaning 'between' or 'middle' – *'meson'*. It would only take a moment's carelessness by a tired scribe to substitute one for the other in error, so perhaps what was actually meant was that Atlantis was 'between Europe and Libya'. This would fit with the presumed identity of the Minoan culture as the main source of Plato's Atlantis.

Similarly, he points out that in ancient times when the horizons of geographical knowledge were more limited, the Pillars of Heracles were not at the Straits of Gibraltar as later thought, but merely Cape Tainaron and Malea on two promontories jutting out towards Crete from the Peloponnesian peninsular.

It is not possible to do justice here to all of Castleden's hypotheses, but he makes a very persuasive case for his view that Minoan Crete and its neighbouring territories were one of the chief ingredients of the Platonic Atlantis.

ATLANTIS AND TROY

Another plausible theory about the identity of Atlantis has recently been well argued by the German geoarchaeologist Eberhard Zangger in *The Flood from Heaven*. He claims that the Atlantis story that Solon picked up in Egypt is nothing more than an unfamiliar description of the great city of Troy, which legend says was destroyed after ten long years of siege by a Greek alliance. As with Castleden's hypothesis, Zangger believes that the account given of Atlantis and ancient Athens to Solon by the Egyptian priest is basically factual, and that any apparent discrepancies can be attributed to language difficulties. Also like Castleden, Zangger assumes that the date given by the Egyptian priest is generally misunderstood to signify solar years when they are actually short 'lunar years'. When corrected, this places the Atlantis story within the late Bronze Age (1400–1150 BCE). Accordingly, he maintains that the basic cultural and technological picture presented by Plato corresponds to the late Bronze Age period and that it is actually quite accurate down to surprisingly small details. He notes a number of factual observations made by the Egyptian priest at the beginning of his conversation with Solon about the antiquity of the Greeks and the disasters that befell them.

Periodic Destruction of Greek Society

The priest stated that the lands of Greece were subject to periodic devastation by floods and other disasters, and this has indeed been corroborated by archaeological research on the ancient Mycenaean sites where whole cities were washed away by flash-floods around 1200 BCE. The traces of devastating flood damage have been found at Tiryns, Mycenae and Midea were destroyed by fires and earthquakes, and Pylos by fire. These floods do not seem to have been caused by the tsunami that occur after earthquakes, but were the lesser-known phenomenon of flash-floods that also occur with earthquakes as rivers are diverted from their channels.

The priest was also aware that the Greeks had mastered the art of writing in former times, but lost the ability for a time before rediscovering it. This again corresponds with the existence of inscriptions in the famous Linear B script found on Crete and the Greek mainland which was only deciphered in the 1950s by the young scholar Michael Ventris. When Greece entered a Dark Age after the collapse of Mycenaean society, the use of Linear B script completely disappeared and the Greeks remained without writing for hundreds of years until it was reintroduced from the Near East around the 7th century BCE. The priest also stated that these periodic floods swept away the cities and their cultured inhabitants while the herdsmen and shepherds in the hills survived. This is reflected in the two epics attributed to Homer, the *Iliad* and the *Odyssey*. When the characters appearing in the *Iliad* and the *Odyssey* are compared, you cannot fail to notice that the former is filled with fierce Greek warrior-nobles and their companions, while the latter features rather more humble plebeians such as artisans and shepherds.

The Location of Atlantis and Troy

Zangger also ties the events related by the Egyptian priest to known archaeological facts. According to the priest, there was a war between Atlantis and Athens in which Atlantis was defeated, but almost immediately afterwards Atlantis and many of the Greeks were destroyed by water. Most of the details that the priest gave about the structure and fate of ancient 'Athenian' or Greek society are accurate and correspond with late Bronze Age Greece.

So one half of the equation seems possible, but how does he connect Troy with Atlantis? The key points given by Plato as to the location of Atlantis are that it is an island, it is in the Atlantic Ocean, it is larger than Libya and Asia together, and it lies within a strait that is difficult to navigate. The last two points are quite compatible with Troy which is located on the eastern side of the Dardanelles Strait, to this day notoriously difficult to navigate. Zangger suggests that the term 'island' in the account arose through linguistic difficulties – since there were no real islands within Egyptian territory, they did not have an explicit word for the concept and so the hieroglyph often translated as 'island' merely means 'a sandy tract' or 'shore'. And when the text says that Atlantis was larger than Libya and Asia, Zangger cites scholarly evidence to demonstrate that this is a Greek idiom which actually means 'of greater significance' than Libya and Asia.

Finally, any reference to the Pillars of Heracles is ambiguous as Castleden also mentions. Even as late as the 5th century, the Roman writer Servius stated, 'We pass through the Pillars of Heracles in the Black Sea as well as in Spain'. Zangger takes the view that the Pillars of Heracles originally denoted a location within the sphere of knowledge of the ancient Greeks – at the entrance to the Black Sea which is, of course, where Troy was located.

Atlantean and Trojan Parallels

In the course of Plato's account of Atlantis, he outlines the genealogical descent of the Atlanteans from Atlas, one of Poseidon's sons. It is therefore striking that a similar genealogy is attributed to the Trojans in the *Iliad*, where it is stated that the Trojan royal lineage also traced their origins to Atlas. Even more noteworthy is the fact that several ancient writers referred to the Trojans as Atlanteans by virtue of their illustrious ancestor. Not a great deal is known about the structure of Trojan society around the time of the Trojan War, but the *Odyssey* states that they were ruled by the aged king Priam. Given the power that Troy undoubtedly wielded in the area, it is possible that they would have established a confederacy of kings, just as Plato states, for such was the norm in ancient times.

Plato's description of his extremely wealthy and aggressive Atlantean nation fits well with our knowledge of politics in the eastern Mediterranean during the late Bronze Age. Troy would have occupied a key position in controlling trade between the Aegean and the Black Sea, if not throughout the whole area. Some scholars have seen the true origin of the Trojan War in Greek resentment at Troy's wealth and monopolistic control over trade, though it is unfortunate that precise dates cannot be given for the Trojan War from the archaeological evidence garnered at the site of Troy. It is known, however, that there were at least two major events of destruction between 1250 and 1200 BCE which may be suitable candidates for the story of the Greek Trojan War. There are also traces of massive destruction and flooding caused by earthquakes shortly after this period when the entire lower part of the city was swept away into the sea.

Zangger describes at length various features known from archaeology that further strengthen his identification of Troy as the true location of Atlantis, and shows that there are a number of distinctive topographical features that tie the two together. He notes that there are considerable points of correspondence in the layout of the capital of Atlantis and of Troy, with the same plain surrounding the city, the same canals and citadel on a low hill. Again, I cannot do full justice to Zangger's detailed arguments in the space of this book, however I do urge you to examine for yourselves what I believe is one of the most rational and plausible theories as to the location of Atlantis, which rivals Castleden's Minoan theory.

Zangger does have one interesting observation with which we may close this chapter. It has often puzzled scholars why Plato never completed the *Critias*. The reason may be quite simple: as Plato progressed with his account of Athens and Atlantis, he may have suddenly realised that this was not the unique story he originally thought, but merely an account of the Trojan War viewed from the Egyptian perspective!

6

ATLANTIS IN THE NEW WORLD

ATLANTIS IN SOUTH AMERICA?

In their search for the location of Atlantis, many seekers draw on specialist or professional skills. One such person is Jim Allen, a former RAF photographic interpreter. Using his expertise with maps and topography, he has recently outlined a novel idea in his *Atlantis: The Andes Solution* regarding the true site of Atlantis: the Altiplano of Bolivia. Whether he has succeeded where all else have failed remains to be seen. Certainly his hypothesis is intriguing, although some of his arguments are suspect. Like many of his predecessors, he was initially attracted to the similarity of words from South American languages, like 'atl' – 'water' – and the first few letters of Atlantis. Indeed, he lists a number of words from Nahuatl, the language of the Aztecs, such as 'tamatatl', 'chocolatl' and 'Quetzalcoatl'. Unfortunately, this is merely a trap for non-linguists since the *–atl* ending of these words has no particular significance – it is merely the standard singular noun ending, so this suffix will inevitably be very common. He then compounds the confusion by pointing out that the native Quechua word for the Andes is *'antis'* or 'copper', and links this with the Nahuatl *'atl'* to yield Atlantis. The problem here is that Nahuatl was the official language of the Aztecs and Quechua of the Incas, two totally different languages and cultures separated by hundreds of miles.

The Altiplano and Atlantis

Be that as it may, Allen pinpoints several key features of Plato's account which led him to identify the Altiplano as the location of Atlantis. First, he rightly points out that Plato's description specifies a rectilinear plain located in the middle of the continent of Atlantis but adjacent to the ocean, that this plain extended lengthways along the longest side of the continent, and was very smooth and level but was surrounded by mountains on all sides. He claims that this description best fits the Bolivian Altiplano since it is a vast level plain which has a unique rectangular shape.

The Altiplano is also endowed with two large bodies of water, the Lakes Titicaca and Poopo. Allen believes that Plato's account may be distorted with regards to the destruction of Atlantis. The text itself is a little confused in its descriptions since it refers to both the land and the capital city as Atlantis. Allen wonders whether it was not the whole continent that sank but merely the capital city. If Atlantis was located on the Altiplano, it is then possible that the city of Atlantis was submerged beneath the waters of Lake Poopo.

He also suggests that a torrential downpour of rain triggered the sequence of events that led to the destruction of Atlantis. If the Altiplano was indeed the site of Atlantis this would fit very well, for the plain itself is completely boxed in by high mountains which effectively trap all water within their confines. It is quite possible that rain was involved but that is not what Plato himself said. Regrettably, Allen relies on a 'translation' prepared by Ignatius Donnelly which has spuriously inserted the word 'rain' in the sentence: 'there occurred portentous earthquakes and floods'. Aside from this Allen reminds us that this region of South America is especially prone to earthquakes and volcanic activity.

In his account of Atlantis, Plato emphasises the wealth of the Atlanteans and particularly mentions their custom of sheathing walls with various valuable metals such as gold, silver, copper and tin. The region of South America described by Allen is famed for its huge deposits of metal ores that have been mined since ancient times. Thus the nearby mountain of Potosi has produced vast quantities of silver and tin, while gold is mined in other neighbouring areas. It is known that the Incas covered many of the walls of their houses and temples with gold and silver, while the buildings themselves were often filled with costly statues of gold. It was, of course, this inconceivable wealth that first attracted the interest of the Spanish in the 16th century.

The Canal System

Allen also draws parallels between the extensive canal system that he identified on the Altiplano, and Plato's Atlantis. The Atlantean canal system featured a huge central canal which was said to be one stade or 600 feet in width. Thus Allen was undoubtedly elated to find that satellite and aerial photographs seemed to show something that looked suspiciously like this very canal in the Altiplano region. A later ground survey in 1995 confirmed the existence of an enormous canal-like construction which is exactly 600 feet in width from the tops of each embankment. The whole area around this large canal is also neatly criss-crossed with smaller subsidiary irrigation canals that form a chequered pattern, just as Plato described on the plain around the capital of Atlantis.

Like many other researchers, Allen finds the enormous linear measurements for this area of irrigation given by Plato somewhat problematic. He suggests that the basic unit of measurement, the stade, that Plato uses throughout his account of the layout of Atlantis, is again based on a faulty transmission of terminology from the Egyptian or pre-Egyptian sources to Plato via Solon. Naturally, a distance of 600 feet is understood as the equivalent of one

Greek stade but Allen thinks that the underlying unit should actually be a half-stade or just 300 feet. However, it is the ratio of the rectangular area of the irrigation canals that is important: 3000:2000. These proportions would fit very well if such a grid were to be laid over the flat Altiplano plain. Such an irrigation system would have been essential to maintain life in this arid region since annual rainfall is normally under five inches per year, though the vast Lake Titicaca to the north would have been a viable source of ample supplies of fresh water. Indeed, the early inhabitants of this plateau seem to have constructed their canal system to irrigate their land with water ultimately derived from Lake Titicaca, which would have held an even greater volume of water in ancient times.

The existence of a scheme on this scale should not be too surprising since the various ancient cultures of South and Central America were great masters of waterway construction, as is known from the Spanish accounts of Tenochtitlan in Mexico. In fact, Allen suggests that the Aztecs, whom he identifies as Atlantean survivors, built this Venice of South America in memory of their lost home.

The Destruction of Atlantis

Allen then goes on to deal with the dating question and how the Atlantis story ended up in Egypt. Like the majority of researchers who wish to be taken seriously, he reduces the key date of Atlantis from Plato's 9,000 years before Solon down to around 730 years by means of the lunar mini-years described. This gives a date in the region of 1300 BCE, which is in agreement with the theories of Castleden and Zangger. Allen believes that his Bolivian city of Atlantis, located on the Altiplano near to Lake Poopo, was destroyed by a cataclysmic downpour of rain, possibly with accompanying earthquakes. If this city were to be found now, archaeologists would need to excavate through the dense salty silt that has accumulated at Lake Poopo.

I believe that this is one of the prime weaknesses of Allen's theory: there does not seem to have been any archaeological investigation in the vicinity that might provide artefacts that could be dated by Carbon 14 or dendrochronological tests to prove his theory. Naturally, Allen needs to have a fairly ancient date for his ideas to work but there seems to be little evidence for extremely early human inhabitation of this part of the Altiplano.

It is also curious that he never mentions the remains of the city of Tiwanaku which lie in this region between Lake Titicaca and Lake Poopo. This impressive ancient site was built by the people of the Pukara culture from around 200 CE onwards until a gradual decrease in rainfall led to its being abandoned around 1000 CE. Given the size of Tiwanaku and its satellite settlements, it is more likely that Allen has identified the irrigation system for the agricultural land that fed the Pukara people rather than any Atlantean remains.

◎   *The Fate of the South American Atlanteans*

Taking his approximate date for the catastrophe that destroyed Atlantis, Allen goes on to suggest how the account of Atlantis ended up in Egypt. Following the destruction of their city, his Atlantean survivors dispersed in different directions. Playing on the idea of the mythical Aztlan homeland of the Aztecs discussed in Chapter 3, Allen believes that some survivors migrated northwards to Mexico where they eventually became the Aztec nation. Other survivors, he says, made their way across the Atlantic to settle, although he indicates that his Atlanteans were already trading with Europe before the destruction of Atlantis in South America.

Allen asserts that the ancient Atlanteans and their partners were engaged in regular transatlantic trade with the Old World, shipping over large quantities of gold and silver from the Atlantic coast of South America. Recalling the joint trips that Kings Solomon and Hiram sponsored to the port of mysterious Tartessus, Allen surmises that Tartessus was an Atlantean port located on the River Plate, while at the European end was the city of Gades in present-day Spain. It is from this trade that these cities derived their enormous wealth in ancient times, and it also accounts for the Phoenician secrecy about what lay beyond the Pillars of Heracles.

Whether prior to the destruction of Atlantis or after is not clear, but the Atlanteans established a number of colonies in various parts of the Mediterranean, such as the

Minoan culture centred on Crete. It was they who formed the marauders known as the Sea People who were active around 1200 BCE and were defeated by the Egyptians. Some survivors of the war were given land by the pharaohs and settled in Egypt, and it must have been through them that the account of Atlantis, albeit in a somewhat distorted form, was preserved in the Egyptian archives.

EDGAR CAYCE

Another theory suggesting that the location of Atlantis is in the New World has surfaced in popular imagination in recent years: Atlantis in the Bahamas.

To place this theory in context we need to go back to the 1930s and consider the psychic 'readings' of Edgar Cayce. A clairvoyant and healer of some talent, Cayce (1877–1945) was born on a small farm in Kentucky. At an early age he did not need to study as normal children do, but had the ability to absorb knowledge from his school books as he dozed head down on them. As a young adult, he developed a strange paralysis of the throat which prevented him from speaking. The doctors were puzzled by this ailment and could offer no diagnosis, but Cayce went into one of his hypnotic slumbers and was able to recommend a cure that proved successful. Not only was he able to cure himself in this manner but he also found that he had the ability to cure other people in the same way. Cayce worked for many years as a clairvoyant healer but branched out later in his life and began making pronouncements on a wide range of topics that are still studied eagerly to this day.

The Atlantean Readings

Among his vast collection of 'readings', which exceed 14,000 in number, there are hundreds dealing with the ancient civilisations of Atlantis and Egypt. Many features of his ideas about Atlantis resemble a combination of the writing of Blavatskian Theosophists and Ignatius Donnelly. He thought that the ancient Atlanteans lived on a continent located in the Atlantic Ocean and that they were an extremely advanced society in terms of technology. However, this technological mastery caused many Atlanteans to lose sight of the spiritual and thus they became immersed in the quest for power and material wealth. This brought about two distinct factions among the Atlanteans: the Children of the Law of One, and the Sons of Belial, who each pursued diametrically opposed paths of development. Those who focused on power and materialism brought about a series of three catastrophes. The first occurred around 50,000 BCE and destroyed the major source of their material power; the second, around 28,000 BCE, resulted in the continent of Atlantis breaking up into three smaller islands of Poseidia, Og and Aryan. A third and final cataclysm occurred around

9,500 BCE, as Plato recounts, which caused these three residual islands to sink below the waves, forcing the survivors to seek refuge in other parts of the world.

The Atlantean Contribution to Civilisation

Fortunately, the more spiritually advanced of the Atlanteans had some prescience of this disaster and were able to migrate safely to Egypt. It was through their influence that Egypt made many great advances in all areas of science and technology. Cayce stated that there was also a spiritual component to their benign influence, for, with the help of these Atlantean refugees, a high priest called Ra Ta instituted a programme of social reform based on concepts of equality, personal transformation and moral responsibility for others. These crucial spiritual developments then found their way into later neighbouring cultures.

According to Cayce, various records and traces of this ancient Atlantean civilisation have survived in a number of parts of the world. Naturally, some are to be found in Egypt, while others, Cayce said, will be found in the Yucatan peninsular, courtesy of the Maya. Most startling of all was Cayce's prediction that remains of Atlantis would begin to resurface in the Bahamas, specifically near the Bimini Islands. Moreover, Cayce's psychic readings foretold that the Biminian remains would first be detected in 1967 or 1968.

Atlantis Resurgens?

It was thus quite astonishing when a pilot in a private plane flying over the Bimini Islands in 1968 noticed from the air an anomalous structure below the surface of the sea. This phenomenon lies less than one mile off the shore of North Bimini at a shallow depth of less than three fathoms. It basically comprises two sets of adjacent rectangular stones laid out in straight parallel rows. In the eyes of the converted, these two linear sets of stones are nothing less than the remains of an ancient roadway, doubtless part of Atlantis beginning to rise as Cayce predicted more than thirty years before.

The area soon attracted great attention from divers and other seekers vying to be the first to confirm the identity of this new location of Atlantis. Some people were so eager that they even lent a helping hand in embroidering the rumour. Aaron Duval of the Egyptological Society of Miami claimed in 1997 to have located megalithic ruins and metal-covered walls with Egyptian-style masons' marks and star charts, among other things. Duval announced that he was going to present his conclusive Atlantean evidence in July 1997 but regrettably he had to cancel or rather postpone this press conference to a later date. Nothing more has been heard since of this development.

Atlantis Sunk Again?

Unless Aaron Duval chooses to make his discoveries public, his theories must sadly be dismissed as rather dubious. This may well be the case, since some people have clearly been planting evidence on the sea-bed. On one occasion, a professional underwater archaeologist was asked to look at a large granite block in the sea off Bimini which apparently had a pyramid carved on its surface. However, the block had almost certainly been deposited there only a very short while beforehand, since it had neither coral growths on it nor had it settled down into the deep silt as would be expected. As for the famous Bimini 'road' itself, the consensus among responsible marine geologists and archaeologists is that the phenomenon is entirely natural. In fact, the limestone rock formations in that area have a natural tendency to fracture into regular blocks just like those making up the 'road'. Besides, if there were truly an underground city along the lines claimed, it would have been found by the US Navy some time ago since they have a very intensive surveillance system operating in this strategically important area and have mapped every inch for the convenience of their submarine training school in the Bahamas.

Of course, the die-hard Atlantis believers do not accept this. They counter that the structure is man-made, and suggest that if the rock in this area fractures in this way by itself, then the Atlanteans would have reasonably made use of the ready-made blocks for their building programmes. More radically, some believe that the US Government has definitively located the lost remains of Atlantis and its technologically advanced artefacts in the Bimini area, but is hiding the discovery so that they can appropriate the technology for military purposes.

It should also be mentioned here that a similar 'megalithic' structure has been discovered off the Japanese island of Yonaguni to the south of Okinawa and greeted with just as much excitement, since it too is thought by some to be the partial remains of an Atlantean city. Sadly, this strange phenomenon can be adequately explained by conventional geological mechanisms, rather like the Giants Causeway located on the shores of Northern Ireland.

7

THE CRADLE OF CIVILISATION

THE SEARCH GOES ON

Almost every conceivable place on earth has at some time been suggested as the site of the original Atlantis, including the Celtic Shelf, the Arctic, Ethiopia, the Caspian Sea, Nigeria, Tunisia, Belgium, the Caucasus and Brazil. Since the arguments offered for the location of Atlantis in these places have generally proved spurious, there are not a lot of places left where it could have existed, though little interest has yet been shown in China or Japan as potential candidates.

I should now like to consider two theories which have a seemingly similar premise as their starting point but then lead in very different directions, both figuratively and literally. These are the hypotheses of Graham Hancock and Stephen Oppenheimer who, respectively, suggest we look at the Antarctic and Sundaland, though neither of them explicitly state that their chosen region was actually the Atlantis of Plato. Each of these writers, in their own way, is a diffusionist; that is to say, they both believe that there was an advanced civilisation somewhere on earth in the distant past from where the transmission of important cultural advances emanated.

The best-selling author Graham Hancock began his career as a freelance journalist, and wrote some serious works on the problems of poverty, famine and AIDS. He then began a series of books on various aspects of the ancient world, accompanied by his unorthodox explanatory theories. Two of his books in particular deal directly with the theme of Atlantis: *Fingerprints of the Gods* and *Heaven's Mirror*. Due to the wealth of information these two books contain, it would be difficult to cover every aspect of his theories, so I shall briefly present two or three of the most salient points here so that you can get a feel for his approach.

THE PIRI REIS MAP

The best starting point is where Hancock himself seems to have started: the Piri Reis Map. This map was compiled in 1513 by the Ottoman Turkish Admiral, Piri Reis, after whom it is now named. Soon after his death in 1555 it was presumably shelved, to lie gathering dust for centuries until it was rediscovered in the Topkapi Place Library in Istanbul in 1929. Even then, it did not attract

much interest until the early 1960s when the American
Charles Hapgood published a series of books with startling revelations about the map, beginning with *Maps of
the Ancient Sea Kings*.

It was thought by Hapgood, and accepted by Hancock,
that the Piri Reis map shows the western coast of Africa,
the eastern coast of South America and the northern coast
of Antarctica. The Antarctica portion also shows an ice-
free Queen Maud Land, even though the last possible ice-
free period would have been no later than 4000 BCE.
Furthermore, Admiral Piri Reis could not have known
about Antarctica from his contemporary sources since
Antarctica was not discovered until 1818.

Based on these facts, Hapgood then arrived at certain
interesting conclusions. First, it is known from annota-
tions on the map in Piri Reis's own handwriting that he
utilised a large number of source maps which he copied
and compiled to make his map. Certainly, as Admiral to
the Ottoman Turks, Piri Reis would have had access to
many maps, some of great antiquity, in the state archives
of Istanbul. Hapgood argued that these ancient maps
themselves must have been based on still older maps and
so on back in time. Hapgood, and thus Hancock, asserted
that based on the Antarctica data presented by Piri Reis,
the world must have been completely mapped some time
prior to 4000 BCE by 'a hitherto unknown and undiscov-
ered civilisation which had achieved a high level of technological advancement'.

Even more startling was Hapgood's theory about shifts

in the earth's crust during the Ice Ages. He maintained that periodically the relatively thin crust of the earth, which floats on the viscous molten mantle, shifts 'like the loose skin of an orange' because of the weight and inertia of the dense masses of ice that build up during an Ice Age. In this way, the ice-free regions of the Antarctic shown on the Piri Reis Map can be explained: prior to 4000 BCE, the Antarctic continent was offset by some 2,000 miles from the South Pole but moved into its present position as a result of this 'earth crust displacement'.

Graham Hancock seizes on Hapgood's work and makes it the cornerstone of his *Fingerprints of the Gods*. He is a little more circumspect in *Heaven's Mirror*, though he still apparently believes that the Antarctic was the home of his Atlantean super-civilisation. Hapgood's theories were not accepted in the scientific community, though Hancock claims that 'none has succeeded in proving it incorrect'.

Cartographical Fictions

Since Hapgood maintained that the Piri Reis map was too accurate to have been compiled by 16th-century cartographers, he tried to prove this by replotting the map in segments on to four separate grids. There are several problems with this, however. The segments are not drawn to the same scale and two of them are rotated by 79° and 40° respectively. Additionally, Hapgood has had to include five different equators on his main and subsidiary grids. There is also a stylised chain of mountains depicted running down the coast of South America in the Piri Reis original which Hapgood asserts are the Andes and thus further proof of the accuracy of the map; they are, however, approximately 1,000 miles too far east. It should also be noted that the South American continent is not drawn separately from the purported Antarctic but joins on to it in a broad sweep. In fact, to produce his modern projection of the Piri Reis map, Hapgood had to make an unjustifiable number of assumptions and subtle alterations of his own, but still the Antarctic portion does not correspond to any land mass in reality.

There is another likely explanation for the presence of an Antarctic-like land mass at the South Pole. Quite simply, ancient Classical geographers came to the conclusion that there must be a land mass in that region on purely logical grounds. They accepted that the earth was a sphere spinning in space and believed that it needed a symmetrical and balanced amount of land distributed on its surface in order for it to remain in equilibrium and to rotate properly. Since they knew much of the northern hemisphere, from the frozen wastes of the north, through Eurasia and Africa and down to the equator, they hypothesised that there had to be similar antipodean land masses. This concept was depicted by the Greek cartographer Ptolomy who joined Africa to east Asia, forming a large continent that he labelled 'Terra Incognita'. Thereafter, this concept was accepted and depicted in some form by virtually all cartographers right up until the 18th-century voyages of Captain Cook which failed to find it.

If we look again at the Piri Reis 'Antarctic', we can see that it is probably no more than an imaginative sketch of the hypothetical southern land mass that all cartographers had included on their maps.

An Ice-bound Continent

Now let us look briefly at what modern geological findings have revealed about Hapgood's assertions concerning the history of the Antarctic. Since the 1950s, the Antarctic has been extensively surveyed and studied by teams of scientists from all over the world, including the former Soviet Union, the United States and Britain. In their researches, many ice-core samples have been extracted and subjected to detailed analysis. Some of the earliest core samples were taken from deep water off the northern Ross Sea and a report on these was published by the geologist Jack Hough in 1950 which identified various types of marine glacial sediment.

When Hapgood read the report he claimed that these glacial deposits were carried down to the sea in the past by ice-free *rivers*, thus proving his theory of an earlier, warmer Antarctic. In fact, Hough's report clearly states these layers of glacial sedimentary deposits were carried there by the Ross Shelf ice shelf which drains over thirty per cent of the Antarctic ice sheet. Not only were the glacial deposits carried there embedded in the ice, but the spread of the marine ice sheet was far greater then than at present – in other words, the Antarctic has not been cooling down over the past 10,000 years; on the contrary, it has been slowly warming up. Other ice-core samples from the land ice show that the Antarctic has been continuously covered with glaciers for anything up to 14 million years, though some geologists argue for a lesser 3 million years! Thus, at no time in the recent past has the Antarctic been a suitable environment for human habitation.

As for the 'earth crust displacement' theory, Hapgood may be forgiven for postulating it 50 years ago when the deep structure of the earth was less well understood, but there is now impeccable evidence that any such movement is utterly impossible. It is known that the crust of the earth is so firmly attached to the upper mantle that there is no possibility that it can move around independently. Though there is a semi-viscous layer about 100–150 kilometres below the earth's surface, it is definitely not fluid enough to permit the kind of rapid movement that Hapgood believed.

So, unless Hancock can disprove this data about the structure of the earth, his hypothetical Atlantis in the Antarctic must be discarded as pure fantasy.

The Sphinx and Leo

Hancock's theory of an ancient super-civilisation is thus damaged but still potentially workable, since he has other findings which he claims indicate a common source for certain ancient architectural features around the world. These are dealt with in detail in *Heaven's Mirror* which, as the title suggests, is particularly concerned with astronomical data. Briefly, Hancock believes that certain noted archaeological sites in Egypt, Cambodia, Mexico, the Pacific and elsewhere, have been laid out to represent various constellations such as Leo, Orion and Draco, as they would have appeared to the observer in 10,500 BCE. Since they all seem to have been laid out on this same principle, they must have been constructed by people who had advanced astronomical knowledge of the skies thousands of years before.

It seems to be the Sphinx at Giza in Egypt which first gave Hancock this idea. He again draws on the opinions of other scholars, in this instance from the amateur Egyptologist John Anthony West. West noted unusual weathering on the body of the Sphinx, which incidentally was carved *in situ* out of a natural outcrop of limestone, which he claimed was the result of water erosion. Since an appreciable amount of rain is now very uncommon in this arid area of Egypt, this water erosion must have occurred in the distant past when the climate around Giza was quite different, possibly between 7,000 to 9,000 years ago according to conventional views, though West and Hancock put this back to more than 10,000 years ago.

Erosion Mechanisms

Though the Sphinx does show some unusual types of erosion, there are other possible explanations that do not seem to have been considered by West and Hancock. And while it is generally accepted that the Giza Plateau region was wetter in the past, current estimates of the annual rainfall for that period are in the region of a mere 10–12 inches of rain per annun – hardly torrential downpours.

A number of geologists have considered the erosion problem and assert that it can be explained by conventional weathering which is caused by the interaction of several phenomena. The whole of the Sphinx is subject to exfoliation due to the capillary action of salt-crystals present in the rock matrix. These salt-crystals absorb moisture from night-time precipitation and, like ice-crystals, cause fragments of the rock to break free and be blown away by the wind. The furrows or striations apparently caused by water erosion could simply be the result of this process working on the natural variations in the limestone material. Additionally, the vertical water-like pattern of erosion could have been accelerated by the inherent joints in the rock that are ubiquitous to Giza Plateau, as well as the processes by which the Egyptians carved out the Sphinx from its matrix.

Hancock also claims that the face on the Sphinx was originally that of a lion which was later recarved by ignorant Egyptians into the face of a pharaoh. He then claims that the mysterious sculptors of the original Sphinx were making a land-based representation of the constellation Leo which would have been viewed on the horizon at the time of the spring equinox in exactly 10,500 BCE. Note however that these sophisticated early astronomer sculptors have left no other traces of themselves; no pottery or bones for the archaeologists to find and date. Regrettably for both Hancock and his opponents, it is impossible to date the carving of the Sphinx precisely since it is a natural rock outcrop.

The Pyramids and Orion

Adopting the ideas outlined in Robert Bauval's *Orion Mystery*, Hancock seeks further corroboration for his theories from the pyramids. When the three pyramids clustered together at Giza near the Sphinx are viewed from above, it will be seen that they lie diagonally, each carefully sited so that they are aligned to the cardinal points. The smaller of the three pyramids, Menkaure, is curiously offset, however. The Belt of Orion in the Orion constellation also reveals the same pattern. It is clear to Hancock that this is quite intentional, a hidden sign for posterity from his lost Antarctic super-civilisation or their descendants. He theorises that Orion was significant to the Egyptians as a portal to the 'other world', since in dynastic times it rose just prior to the sun around the summer solstice and heralded the opening of a gate for the souls of the dead. However, due to the gradual precession of the constellations this was not always the case, hence this phenomenon would have occurred at the spring equinox in 10,500 BCE.

Doubtless, the stars of the night sky held great significance to the ancient Egyptians, but we are in danger of missing Hancock's sleight of hand, for what we do not normally notice is that the Belt of Orion is actually upside-down in the sky in relation to the pyramid layout, and that the degree of offset is incorrect anyway. Surely, his ancient pyramid builders would have noticed this and put the pyramids the right way around on the ground?

There is also another explanation for this offset third pyramid. The small pyramid of Menkaure was the last of the three to have been built and therefore its builders were restricted in their choice of location. In principle, it should have been constructed exactly along the diagonal line created by the two earlier pyramids, however this was not possible for one simple reason: there is an uneven rocky outcrop at that point which rendered the ideal site totally unsuitable. The Egyptian architects had no alternative but to offset the third pyramid in this way, thus creating something that has a passing resemblance to the Belt of Orion when turned upside-down.

SUNDALAND

In all the attempts to find a sunken land that could have been the location of either Plato's Atlantis or at least the home of an advanced ancient culture, it is surprising that geneticist Stephen Oppenheimer is the first scholar to have suggested the one place on earth where vast areas of land were drowned in comparatively recent times. Unfortunately, Oppenheimer's *Eden in the East* is not a glossy, sensational production, so it may not get the attention it deserves. Indeed, Oppenheimer only mentions Atlantis once in passing, but the work is intellectually satisfying since it is largely grounded in solid scientific research ranging from archaeology, linguistics, anthropology and genetic studies. Named after the Sunda Straits, Sundaland is the provisional name given to the vast area of land around offshore South East Asia that was drowned in several phases during the aftermath of the last Ice Age. It once formed a huge continental shelf that joined together the now separate land masses and islands of Malaysia, Sumatra, Java, Borneo, Thailand, Vietnam and parts of China, and which now lies deep below the ocean's surface.

Ice Age Floods

Oppenheimer opens his book with a brief discussion of the flood myths that are found around the world, and the hypothesis that many of them have their origins in the series of catastrophic deluges that occurred as the last Ice Age came to an end. He points out that the gradual melt process and release of the pent-up water reserves did not happen as smoothly as popular belief would have it. In fact, palaeobiological and geological evidence shows that the release of melt water happened in three stages in the past 15,000 years, each causing a rise in sea levels and a subsequent brief period of cooling. The first flood would have happened around 14,000 years ago, the second around 11,000 years ago, and the third just over 7,000 years ago. The third and final flood was probably the greatest flood that has occurred in the past two million years of the earth's history, and was caused by the sudden release of melt water that had built up behind the North American Laurentide ice sheet. As this collapsed, a huge lake of water, estimated by some to have been in excess of 100,000 cubic kilometres of water, poured out through the Hudson Strait. This alone would have been enough to cause the sea levels to rise instantaneously by up to 30 feet.

Indeed, the most recent research on this event indicates that the flooding was even more disastrous than previously imagined. In fact, it seems that as the earth's crust rebounded from the weight of the ice, the sea levels would have risen in excess of 80 feet – some 18 feet higher than at present – followed by a fall after hundreds of years to present-day levels. This was accompanied by wide-spread earthquakes and volcanic activity throughout the world. It can also be assumed that the release of the melt water in North America was accompanied by similar events at other glacier fields around the world and the melting of much surface ice elsewhere. It was also at this time that the rising waters of the Mediterranean burst through the Bosphorus and flooded the extensive basin that now forms the Black Sea. It was this flood that drowned the sub-continent of Sundaland, obliterating all traces of this cradle of human civilisation.

The Neolithic Cradle of Civilisation

The people who once inhabited Sundaland have nothing in common with the fantasy populations of super-advanced beings so beloved of other Atlantean writers and researchers. Nevertheless, they were remarkable by Neolithic standards for it seems from the archaeological record that they were responsible for many key cultural developments in the fields of agriculture, tool-making and, it is thought, religion. They were at the forefront of the Neolithic Agricultural Revolution when domestication of wild foods began in earnest; it is known that these people were using stone querns to grind cereals at least 24,000 years ago. They also cleared land and created terraced plots for growing taro plants, and it was they who first cultivated the Asian staple food, rice. The technologies of megalith construction, the use of bark-cloth and various tools can also be traced to this area. And from the distribution of archaeological evidence left by these people and their immediate descendants throughout the entire region, from China, South East Asia and right across the Western Pacific area, we also know that they were intrepid seafarers, travelling enormous distances over the open seas.

Though they are thought to have been a racially different but contemporary people, the early Jomon inhabitants of Japan were involved in trade with their southern neighbours. Many people are unaware that the earliest known pottery was made by these Jomon people at least 12,000 years ago. Fragments of their pots have been found as far away as Fiji and have been scientifically dated to 6,000 BCE, possibly exported at that time from Japan as luxury items. It was these seafaring skills that probably enabled at least some of the Sundaland inhabitants to flee the rapidly rising flood waters and thus find new homes in many parts of Asia.

Language Families

That these people did migrate thousands of miles away from their drowned homelands can also be proven through linguistics. With the exception of certain isolates, modern world languages can all be classed into related families which have evolved from a single parent language. Some of these have been very well researched, although many difficulties still remain in the precise details of their relationship and development. One of the best known of these language families is Indo-European, which comprises most of the languages of present-day Europe, Iran and northern India. By comparing similarities in common words and basic grammatical structures, it is possible to determine not only which languages are related and the probable era in which they diverged from the parent stock, but also to reconstruct, to a degree, the ancestral forms of common words in the parent ancient language.

One language family that received little attention until the last decade is the Austro-Asiatic group, together with its cousin the Austronesian group. The Austro-Asiatic languages are those spoken by some people in eastern India, such as the Mundas, the Mon-Khmer in Kampuchea, and the Miao in parts of southern China. The Austronesian languages are those of Indonesia,

Borneo, Australia and all the Pacifica islands. There is enough common vocabulary to assume that there was one single ancestral language that gave rise to all the modern languages in these two groups, and judging by the distribution pattern of these languages, it seems clear that the original heartland of this ancestral language is precisely the region where Sundaland once existed. From specialist linguistic data, it follows that the spread of these people through this vast region must have occurred in Neolithic times, and this was undoubtedly triggered by the sudden and devastating floods that destroyed much of the Sundaland region around 7,000 years ago.

The Genetic Evidence

Since he is a geneticist by training, Oppenheimer has also been able to make expert use of genetic data that has been totally ignored by other amateur 'Atlantis hunters'.

All of our physical characteristics are determined by the DNA which we inherited from our parents. At various points in human history, subtle mutations occur in the DNA structure which give rise to variants that are then passed down to all future generations. Though by no means an infallible technique, one can theoretically reconstruct a kind of genetic genealogy for the world population which shows who is related to who and how, by tracking a specific mutation back to its original population, noting that all people who currently have this mutation must also be descended in part from that origin.

Oppenheimer uses several key genetic markers which must have originated in the Sundaland region, such as that associated with beta thalassaemia which gives some protection against malaria.

When Oppenheimer evaluates this genetic data with respect to present-day world populations, the results are astonishing. Naturally, the genetic traits specifically associated with the Sundaland area are now to be found all around that area of Asia, from India to Korea, Burma, and even in Tibet, then right through the island chains of the Pacific from Australia to eastern Polynesia. But it is especially interesting to note that they are also found in Iraq, Turkey, Kurdistan and some areas of the eastern Mediterranean. This clearly demonstrates that the former inhabitants of Sundaland migrated vast distances, bringing their advanced Neolithic culture to their new homes. This is corroborated by archaeological and mythological evidence in a number of regions, such as in the case of the early Sumerian civilisation in the Middle East where there are definite signs of innovative newcomers in the wake of the last great flood of 7,000 years ago.

It might be said, therefore, that we have finally identified the holy grail of the diffusionists, and it was not some fantasy continent in the middle of the Pacific, nor in the Atlantic nor even in the Antarctic. The Neolithic inhabitants of the sunken Eden of Sundaland were neither supermen nor an occult spiritual elite, but the little-known key contributors to all the early developing civilisations in Eurasia, and to whom we are indebted.

8

THE VALUE OF
ATLANTIS

When I look back to my childhood in the late 1950s, I remember long hot summers filled with adventure, and winters when snow fell at the right time; an age when people were kinder, less aggressive and more honest. Yet I also remember my parents complaining about life, and reminiscing about how much better things were when they were young. I was also fortunate enough to meet my aged Victorian great-grandmother and I believe she said the same thing. If you follow this through logically, then at some time in the distant past the world must have been a veritable paradise. But, of course, life was not really that much better in the past, and one could even argue that it was really much worse. On a small scale, my imagined happy era of childhood is nothing more than a myth.

On a grander scale, every human society in the world possesses their collection of myths, whether consciously or unconsciously; the recourse to myths seems to be one of the ubiquitous features of civilisation. Throughout human history, some myths have come and gone, while others have shown remarkable powers of endurance.

In both ancient and modern society, myths have served several purposes. They may be explanatory means to account for the way things are – how the world was created, how humans originated, why we must do certain things and not others. In this sense, myths are an extremely ancient way of transmitting the knowledge that is needed to co-ordinate the functioning of society and to reinforce the common identity of its members. Often there is a definite overlap between myths and religion, though as religions have become formalised and established institutions, there is a tendency to discount the mythic quality of beliefs and to treat them as literal truths. Perhaps this is the purpose of a myth – to be so persuasive that we take it at face value and believe in it literally.

Other myths are a little different. They do not so much explain as provide an example. They offer a paradigm of behaviour that we are encouraged to accept and uphold in our own lives. Perhaps some of these myths were consciously created by early social or religious leaders as a way of lifting society towards a cherished ideal. This has clearly been extremely effective in the past and continues to be so in the present. Sometimes, a myth of this sort can have a very benign effect on society, while others have led to the most appalling atrocities, some of which have been experienced in the last hundred years.

In the course of this book, I have outlined the fortunes of one particular myth – that of the lost land of Atlantis and its advanced yet corrupt society. As discussed, it is probable that Plato himself was the author of this myth for he virtually spells this out in the context of his narrative in the *Timaeus* and the *Critias*. He wanted to depict the way in which an early ideal version of Greek society managed to overcome the threat of invasion from a materially and numerically more powerful state. So that his message would have the greatest impact, he seems to have consciously designed the myth so that it would sound convincing in all its details. To this end, it should not be too surprising to find that he drew from material that he had to hand in his own day – earlier myths, travellers' tales and half-remembered accounts of the Minoan and Trojan cultures.

His handiwork has been more successful than he could ever have imagined. Generations of seekers have taken the story literally and devoted enormous amounts of energy and time in their quest for the location of the lost land of Atlantis. Yet it is so typical of our culture that very many of those seekers have focused on the material aspect rather than the spiritual side of the Atlantis story. Indeed, most have quite missed the point for they have concentrated on the wrong part of the myth – they have been concerned with finding the lost home of the villains of the story, when they should have been trying to establish a kind of society like that of the ancient Athenians, which Plato praises and holds up as a model for us.

Some writers have even abandoned all attempts to locate Atlantis in terms of Plato's description, and have instead tried to find the ancient homeland of a race of people endowed with advanced scientific and cultural achievements, though they still call it Atlantis. Perhaps conditioned by the type of childhood memories that I mentioned above, they are seeking a modern form of the Garden of Eden, an ancient paradise on earth that has been lost forever through humanity's wrong-doing. Often this class of Atlantean writer makes use of other myths drawn from all over the world. Their approach is usually along the lines of the ancient Greek historian Euhemerus, a man before his time, for as we have seen he was the first person known to have sought a rational explanation for myths.

I would not deny that there is every chance that some myths have their basis in fact – the ubiquitous flood myths are good examples of this. This approach can lead to some interesting results and throw light on human prehistory, but at the same time it seems to miss the point. The power of myths lies not in their basis in fact but in their tremendous power to inspire and guide us.

If we want to understand the significance of Plato's Atlantis myth, we should think of how society is structured. If we believe that there was a Golden Age in the past or that there could be one in the future, then we should stop looking for the illusory traces of a non-existent Atlantis and instead try to understand how we can change our own society so that it becomes more just.

FURTHER READING

PRIMARY SOURCES
The Timaeus and the Critias, trans. Bury, R.G. (1929) Harvard
  University Press
The Timaeus and the Critias, trans. Taylor, Thomas (1944) Pantheon
  Books
Timaeus and Critias, trans. Lee, Desmond (1971) Penguin Books
Diodorus of Sicily, trans. Oldfather, C.H. (1967) 12 vols, Heinemann

SECONDARY LITERATURE
Allen, J.M. (1998) *Atlantis, The Andes Solution*, Windrush Press
Blavatsky, Helene (1888), *The Secret Doctrine*, 12 vols, Theosophical
  Publishing House
Calvo, T. and Brisson, L. eds. (1997), *Interpreting the Timaeus-Critias*,
  Sankt Augustin
Castleden, Rodney (1998) *Atlantis Destroyed*, Routledge
Churchward, James (1926), *The Lost Continent of Mu*, Washburn
Donnelly, Ignatius, (1882), *Atlantis: The Antediluvian World*, Harper
Hancock, Graham (1995), *Fingerprints of the Gods*, Heinemann
Landa, Diego de (1941), *Landa's Relacion de las Cosas de Yucatan*,
  Peabody Museum
Le Plongeon, Augustus, (1896), *Queen Moo & the Egyptian Sphinx*,
  Kegan Paul
Levi, Peter (1980), *Atlas of the Greek World*, Phaidon Press
Morgan, K.A. (1998) 'Designer history: Plato's Atlantis story and
  fourth-century ideology', *JHS* 118 (1998) 101–118.
Oppenheimer, Stephen (1998) *Eden in the East*, Weidenfeld &
  Nicholson
Sprague de Camp, L. (1970), *Lost Continents*, Dover Publications
Zangger, Eberhard (1984) *The Flood from Heaven*, Sidgwick & Jackson

INDEX